NORFOLK

Edited by Michelle Warrington

First published in Great Britain in 1999 by
POETRY NOW YOUNG WRITERS
Remus House
Coltsfoot Drive
Woodston
Peterborough
PE2 9JX

Telephone 01733 890066

HB ISBN 0 75430 391 8
SB ISBN 0 75430 392 6

FOREWORD

This year, the Poetry Now Young Writers' Kaleidoscope competition proudly presents the best poetic contributions from over 32,000 up-and-coming writers nationwide.

Successful in continuing our aim of promoting writing and creativity in children, each regional anthology displays the inventive and original writing talents of 11-18 year old poets. Imaginative, thoughtful, often humorous, *Kaleidoscope Norfolk* provides a captivating insight into the issues and opinions important to today's young generation.

The task of editing inevitably proved challenging, but was nevertheless enjoyable thanks to the quality of entries received. The thought, effort and hard work put into each poem impressed and inspired us all. We hope you are as pleased as we are with the final result and that you continue to enjoy *Kaleidoscope Norfolk* for years to come.

CONTENTS

Emily Harrison	87
Zoe Mellor	88
Keith Paler	88
Charlotte Walters	89
Robert Harwood	90
Michael Balls	90
Michael Gricks	91
Claire Bishop	92
Tim Weller	92
Cathy Norton	93
Hazel Gray-Read	93
Jodie McMahon	94
Chris James	94
Sammie Stygall	95
Samantha Dingle	95
Stephanie Allen	96
Rebecca Rump-Smith	96
Ashley Curtis	97
Darryl Clarke	97
Leah Hartwell	98
Sarah Hardwick	99
Ben Timewell	99
Jennifer Anne Stacey	99
Jennifer Coward	100
James Mason	100
Rebecca Mileham	100
Andrew Heath	101
Glen Coston	101
Joe Hender	101
Kira Talbot	102
Oliver Burrage	102
Amy Simmons	103
Dominic Gilham	103
Lauren Emmerson	103
Danielle Stanley	104
Danielle Coulam	104
Jenny Weeks	104
Peter Scrivener	105

Methwold High School

The Poems

JULIE CANE

Here lies the body of Julie Cane,
All through her life she stayed the same,
All the selfishness she had,
All the things that she thought bad,
Every single day went by,
Feeling low or feeling high,
Spiders were her greatest fear,
She'd scream so much she'd flood out tears,
Her selfishness brought her down,
She'd be a queen who wore a crown,
Why'd she have to be so cruel?
Why'd she have to be a fool?
People admired her beauty,
But not her personality,
She died of cancer what a shame,
Wanted to be rich and have fame,
Her death was not a big surprise,
Her life was full of truth and lies,
She'll never see the light of day,
I have nothing else left to say!

Sarah Mehran

MY SECRET PLACE

My secret place
is
a blue box
left over
from moving house.
It is damp
soggy
and falling apart.
As I go in
I feel
a wave of happiness
relief
and joy.
It has a damp smell
of wood,
rotting.
As I close my eyes
I travel into
a garden
made of happiness
love
and peace.
There are birds
animals
and plants.
Ripe fruit grows
on every tree.
The stream is cool
and clear
like ice.
Nothing is real.

It is a sort of
dream.
Nobody else is there
Just me.
Nothing can hurt me.
There is never anger
or pain.
But I know
that if I go to sleep
the dream will disappear.

Catherine Victoria Wozniakowski

A STORM

The strong storm,
Is an angry sky.
Whirling around you, like a waltzer at a fairground.
Whooshing
Whirling
Wind
Hits you like a bad thought
Stinging like a bee.
Lightning lashes out from the sky,
Like a bullet from a gun.
Sound of rain,
Running
Rushing feet.
Cackling heard above,
Witches laughing.
The storm slows,
Until it stops.
Giving a sigh,
Of relief.

Jenna Haddaway (13)
Acle High School

SPIDER'S WEB

'An Englishman's home is his castle.'

The King of a castle
In the clouds.
The keeper
Of the dungeons,
Guards his home
A palace,
Drenched
In tears of morning dew
Like priceless crystals
Delicately
Placed on a silver chain.

The woven web of passages
The London underground
Without the wait.
Flickering in the wind,
Like a candle struggling
For survival.

The fine thread
Sticky as candyfloss
Delicate as china.
Creates a haven hidden
Among a forest of plants.

A death trap,
A kitchen,
A bedroom,
A lounge,
A castle.

Nancy Small (14)
Acle High School

THE BLACK CAT

A network of roads with busy minds scurrying
A machine with headlights piercing, purring,
A watchful mother worrying, wearily,
A witch's familiar hurrying,
At the summoning words,
An unlucky beacon
An unwelcome charm.

The black cat seeps,
Through the mists of time,
Light as a feather,
Black as a tunnel.
He winds through a chimney.
A bridal shower of soot,
Meets his unthinkable thoughts of escape.

His piercing eyes
Looking through you,
Searching you.
His eyes holding secrets unseen by others,
An uncharted kingdom
Of lies of time,
An embrace
Of kisses of truth.
A broken mist appears.

He walks on a bed of cotton
Or tap-dances through the streets,
Silky and slippery as a snake,
Fierce, feline, fighting.
A winding ball of fun.

He greets a phoenix sky of glory.

Marie Coleman (13)
Acle High School

A RED RIVER

It's a red river flowing through my body
It ripples back and forth to the sea.

Microscopic white fish fight
In the depths with intruders
And work with the red fish
To keep their factory working.

Tens of tributaries and canals
Pumping the river round and round,
In a swirling dizzy motion.

It gives me a burst
The waves in the sea grow huge.

My eyes start to roll, and my knees get weak.
The river to my brain slows to an abrupt halt
The river turns cold
The fish die.

I feel myself fall
Then the river is still and the waves no more.

Lisa Cook (13)
Acle High School

HATE

A kettle boiling
A bomb waiting to go off.

Like a tree,
It grows and grows.
Unless you cut it down.

But still its there,
Tunnelling, channelling.

Growing stronger.
Until it bursts
Through the surface
Piercing the skin.

The earth shudders
Stops
Never to start again.

Nadine McIntosh (13)
Acle High School

TREES

Deep down in the forest all alone,
A mix of green and brown confetti
Flowing from volcanoes.
Huggable statues, grow and grow like love,
Until they reach their ultimate destiny;
Rotting,
Unless they are hacked down in the prime of life,
Like divorce.
Thousands of witches surround you
With creepy claws on the ends of millions of stretchy arms.
The rich colours
So majestic,
Make you feel like millionaires.
At night,
You see so many scary faces,
Almost like you are the innocent one,
In a room of criminals and murders.
Deep down in the forest all alone.

Rachel Creak (13)
Acle High School

TELEVISION

On,
as soon as the button's pressed,
a snake starts to emerge from the glass portal,
as if someone pressed a switch,
so the snake can slither and entwine round you,
squeezing the life away so you have to gasp for breath.

It is a poisonous gas encircling you,
undetectable.
It tracks you down as if it were a hungry wolf, hunting,
ready to make you another lost soul.

It is an electric drug,
wanting you to become a lifeless zombie.

Behind the ever-changing images and the murky glass lies,
a lake, in wait.
Inviting it may seem but,
step into the murky waters and you,
may be dragged down into the once inviting water,
drowning your soul, it will keep you at the bottom of
the lake,
another lifeless corpse.
The reeds are like a maiden's hair, keeping you
tangled, forever.

The only way to get free is to press,
Off!

Eleanor Mallett (13)
Acle High School

DEPRESSION?

I'm depressed, no more no less,
My life in ruins, all plans a mess.
I've never been jolly, I've never been mad,
I've always been like this, which is completely sad.
I had no job and I had no hobbies,
My only option was to become a bobby.
So I carry a truncheon, Wow! Big deal!
You wouldn't laugh if you felt how I feel.
The cap means nothing, no pride no power,
It just gives me a taste, a taste of sour.
At home it's no better, with no one to talk to,
I feel like I'm twisted, like a cork and corkscrew.
When night appears I decide to knock off,
But I toss and I turn, and I sneeze and I cough.
I awake all frozen, feel heavy in the head,
Sometimes is it worth it? I'd rather be dead.
But my heart still keeps pumping, I still move around,
But why look up when you're feeling down?
Time to work again, put pen to paper,
Why is my life like water vapour?
No one sees me, oh why, oh why,
Am I really just background like the clouds in the sky?
People stare at me, stare at my shape,
. . . But beneath is a 'should-be' trying to escape . . .
A few moments later, the shape has changed, It keeps on doing that,
again and again.
More people gaze at my brand new exterior, but am I advanced or am I
inferior?
So many choices, the route is a fuzz. Is there an explanation? Ah yes,
because;
I'm depressed, no more no less, my life in ruins, all plans a mess.

Adam Rednall (14)
Acle High School

A VOLCANO

Standing tall and proud, guarding its territory like a lion,
Guarding its den.
Violent lava bubbling like a witch's cauldron.
Vicious volcano builds up pressure,
Erupts like a lonely child who can't take any more
Torment.
Ferocious flames of fire filled with fury,
Spewing out lava as red as blood.
Lava weaving its way down the mountain like a snake
Slithering through the grass,
Smoke filling the sky.
The ash falls from the darkened sky,
Causing destruction and damage with its might.
Roaring, rumbling, spewing, tumbling.
Creatures flee from the almighty giant.
People scream and shout as the hot liquid
Comes creeping towards them.
Silence as a carpet of ash is laid upon them . . .

Lewis Snitch (13)
Acle High School

DIVORCE

Two raging dragons caress their anger,
Then fire it at the other's heart,
The precious jewel for which they fury,
Cries tears of bewilderment.

The warming shield that raised the infant,
Turned to ice and cracked in two,
Both bees left their only flower,
To die with burnt out hearts.

Although the dragon hunts its mate,
The daughter is the prey,
She's the one, who sees the anger,
Watches her makers tear each other apart.

The jewel is left a foundling,
Lying different sides of her,
A piece of blackened coal.

Vicky Pratt (13)
Acle High School

ARE THEY FRIENDS

Serpents or angels you can
never tell.

Surrounded in their many disguises,
held together with seams of lies and deceit.

Their evil hearts hidden by soft silk
Spun by the dragon itself.

They wait, creep around me,
to steal my precious gems and gold,
and shatter into a hole of meaningless
chatter.

My head hung low towards my hunters

My flower will wither and die

They have taken my diamonds from my
quarry, now I'm worthless.

But I won't die, I'll carry on.
My angels will lift my head high!

Kirsty Culley (13)
Acle High School

CAT

Always ready to pounce
on his quarry,
Silently moving, waiting,
crouching, observant
contemplating ambush.

Despite his infamous behaviour
he is treated like Royalty
at home,
coming and going
when he pleases.

Until he sleeps,
inconspicuous
and no longer exuberant
but dead to the world.

Jaycee Collier (13)
Acle High School

JOEY

You were always there when I was small
A lovely soft feathery blue ball.
I used to hold you and teach you to talk, Joey.
We loved one another just you and me.
Now you are gone up in the big sky
I often think of you when a bird flies by.
I know that you're happy now you are free
To fly with the other birds naturally.
To be shut in a cage must be cruel
But I did love you Joey when I was small.

Lee Gibbs (14)
Acle High School

WAR

Sneaking up like a cat to its prey
War looms closer every day.
Frightened people,
What would become
Of their much beloved son
As he goes out to war?

The promises (all fake)
The super-powers make
Are nothing to us folk,
To some innocent bloke,
As he goes out to war.

Rat-tat-tat go the guns,
Ruthless as the hunt.
Those strutting turkey generals
Say our weapons must not be blunt.
When we go out to war.

The sun is low,
The war shadow long.
Still the chess pieces
Are moved along,
When they are out at war.

It's chalk v cheese, every man for himself,
Potter's dead, so's Smith and Delf.
No one really knows what's best,
Will no one help us in our quest
To put a stop to war?

James Gilder (13)
Acle High School

SUN

The sun shines bright
Like a headlight or an egg yolk
In a frying pan.

The clouds
Around it are those bits of cotton wool
Which warm up a cold baby chick.

Penetrating those clouds
Like a tiger tearing at flesh.
Even though it plays hide and seek
It knows and sees everything.

This defenceless lemon
Is eaten every night
By those evil moon and stars

Burning toast to a crisp,
Crossing the sky like a UFO
Making multicoloured bridges when it rains

This ball of gas
Goes up and down like a yo-yo.

Bringing life
To everything it touches.

Martin Sturman (13)
Acle High School

MY GUITAR

A *roaring* lion,
a singing bird,
whichever one
it must be heard.

Six long snakes
are crawling by,
their *harsh-toned* voice
that fills the sky.

From the king of sound
come invisible fish,
they'll come and catch you
despite your wish.

With its heavenly sound
it seems quite tame,
then come the screams of *hell,*
not quite the same.

A flash of *lightning,*
a striking fork,
the heavy thunder starts to talk.

A branch has snapped,
the tree is *dead,*
the lion is sleeping,
no more shall be said.

Matthew Brown (13)
Acle High School

THE KETTLE

Metal, plastic, gas, electric,
Tall, short, fat, thin,

From the gentle buzz,
To the boiling rampage.

A warmly glowing orange light,
The water heating,
The vapour rising,
Waiting . . .

Now the click,
Like a croc's jaw snapping
whilst looking for prey.
The vapour rising,
The sauna door swung open.

The coiled cable is cooling,
the stampede is over,
now just the pleasure is
Waiting . . .

James Kent (13)
Acle High School

SHARK!

I'm quick and quiet
Like a cat
Moving through
The empty wilderness.

I'm smart and swift
Like a fox
Being chased by
The hunter and his hounds.

I'm mysterious and marvellous
Like a panther
Waiting, waiting still
In the everlasting darkness.

I'm deadly and dangerous
Like a cobra
Striking down
Its defenceless prey.

I'm a shark.

Toby Brown   (13)
Acle High School

GRANDPARENTS

Grandparents,
Are big like whales,
Snoring through their blowholes
On a soft and comfy sea.
Grandparents
Are like squirrels,
Storing and keeping the nuts of uselessness
In a hole in the loft.
Grandparents,
Are like ice-creams
Multi-flavoured, loved by all,
A sugar-centred softness.

Jamie Everest   (13)
Acle High School

THE SUN

At the centre of our universe
It sits in its own position,
Never moving,
Never stirring
It leads us around itself.

We are members of a gang
There are nine of us in all,
Each following our fiery leader
Forever and ever more.

But how did our great God get there?
Through a Big Bang or did it evolve?
Nobody really knows for sure
And they probably never will.

So what will happen to our sun?
Blow up
Or cease to be,
But it will not happen for sometime
So you'll have to wait and see.

Ross Coupland (13)
Acle High School

SKY

The never ending mysterious blue sky,
Turns from blue to black and back again
Puffed up pillows on a nice clean bed
Neatly spread out on the never ending
Mysterious blue sky.

A huge blank wall
With nothing to see but the cracks
Moving in the never ending
Mysterious blue sky!

Lynsey Girling (13)
Acle High School

WASPS

Somewhere in the foliage the wasps stand to attention,
In black and yellow uniforms,
Armed with a mighty stainless steel sting,
Like a thunderbolt thrust into reverse
The wasp is unconquered.

In regiments flying in stealth fighters,
Flaming the skies behind them,
The wasps chant a war song that nobody can understand
With all the speed of a concord and force of a battering ram.
Under the uniform the wasp's body is a chrome-plated tank.

The wasp collects its gold,
Soars into the sky and laughs at the impostors,
The wasp rules the sky, in its lap of honour,
Loops the loop before collecting its Olympic torch.

Each wasp in turn lines up to bring the queen her treasure,
It's a once in a lifetime thing, you might think,
But it's all in a day's work for the wasp.

Jessica Morgan (13)
Acle High School

WATER

A slippery clear crystal smooth at the touch
That slips through your fingers
Like grains of sand.

It is silky velvet fluttering in a summer breeze
And a soft waterfall crashing
Down into an evergreen forest.

The trickle of a gentle
Almost empty stream
To the rough and tumble of the sea.

Roars and races like a lion
But can move as swift
And silent as an owl.

The trickle of water is a robin red breast
Twittering
Away in early spring.

A life giving ray
With a gentle sensation
But with wind

Can mean destruction
Anguish,
And *death*.

Alex McNair (13)
Acle High School

MONEY

Money is power
Money is status
Money is a man's pride and joy.
Money is comfort
Money is wealth
And money is a child's favourite toy.
Money is politics
Money is laws
Money is peace
And money is wars
Money is success
Money is failure
Money sees the rich and the poor
Money is the root of all evil
And a provider for those you adore.
Money is a dream, a nightmare and a strange,
Dark mystery all in one.
And money is the source of what we would -
Call fun.
Money can buy you any object
For which you wish,
But a single emotion it cannot
Money is the reason some people are remembered
And the reason why others forgot.
Money is God,
Looking down on us mortals,
And Satan
Tempting fate to us all.
Money is a mixture of these wondrous things
Be they pleasant, horrible, large or small.

Thomas Cheongvee (13)
Acle High School

BUTTERFLY

Of all the creatures it is the
Queen,
The butterfly,
Graceful, bright, careful

Each one special and different
Like a day of a week.

Graceful,
It is like a swan,
Starts as an ugly duckling,
As a butterfly is a caterpillar
Then . . .
It is a beautiful, graceful
Swan.

Bright
It comes out to brighten up
A summer's day,
The colours so majestic;
From the midnight blue,
So bold,
To the palest cream like yellow,
Which resembles gold.

Careful,
It flies through the air
Carefully,
As a mother holds her baby.

Its precious wings,
Like someone's feelings,
Are fragile.
They'll never go back
Together,
If you break them.

Nicola Andrew (13)
Acle High School

WHITEBOARD

The ever-changing
Stretching white beach,
Cleared
By waves of clear chemical cleaner.
Blue, black,
Red or green seaweed
Strewn in armies across the shores.

Scribbles,
Like lovers initials
Scrawled haphazardly
Along clear beaches,
Later to be destroyed
By small children
Playing teachers.

Teaching the children
How to behave
How to learn
And how to be.
The beach should be explored
Like the sea,
What is the final frontier?

Lucy Booth (13)
Acle High School

SAD CLASS CLOWN

I am the clown
The clown of the class
I am hated by everyone
Hated
But not by myself.

I am a sad clown
Sad like a fish
A lonely fish
The fish that no one wants.

I look stupid
Stupid like a Picasso painting
Artistic and skilled
But stupid

When I die
My funeral will be empty
No one there
No one
At all.

I am the clown
Clown of the class
Lonely
Stupid
Sad
I am a clown.

Jason Bird (14)
Acle High School

THE ROOFTOP MOUNTAINS

Peaks of gravel, grime and stone,
Like the mountains they rise
Above the hubbub of the common world.

The rooftops are the suburban
Version of the mountains.
(Or in human proportions anyway).

The peaks peer over green grass,
And luscious lakes.
The roofs peer over nosy neighbours,
And gabbing grannies.

If I had it my way,
I know I'd be a rooftop,
Talking to the trees,
I'm bored being a mountain.

It's a lonely, lazy job,
People just walk by, oblivious
To my obvious boredom,
To them I'm just an attraction
Of my life,
They've been here a tiny fraction.

Michelle Randall (13)
Acle High School

Earth's Salvation

On a planet deep in solar space,
A soul has bred a vulgar race.
A race of savages, of unemotional slayers,
Who wreck their own lives for the sake of employers.
They live within blinkers, in a world of their own,
Joy has all gone now they exist just to moan.
They've slaughtered and massacred billions a year,
With no remorse or shed of a tear.
They've poisoned the land, the air and the sea,
Who are these creatures?
Well, they're you and me.
Just think what we've got, then think what we had,
A beautiful world that all turned bad.
The natural world massacred, the creatures deprived,
And to think they were stunning 'til mankind arrived.
Man needs more space for population explosion.
So lush green trees go with deforestation.

The eyes of the tiger, ebony black,
Its majestic skin in a poacher's sack.
An elephant's tusk or a rhino's horn.
Brutally hacked at the break of dawn.
The plight of the panda, the hippo and ape,
At the edge of extinction, little hope of escape.
The cry of the whale as it's hunted for meat,
Should haunt us forever and not let us sleep.
We should all speak out, weep as a nation,
And put a stop to the vile devastation.
Each man should hold the next man's hand,
And join together to save this land.

The human race should learn it's not
Colour or creed,
And for Earth's salvation absorb love,
Repel greed!

Erika Chalkley (12)
Caister High School

AMAZING SEAS

The waves of the roaring sea
Sweep the helpless sand away into
the depths of a magical land of
life and wonders.

Down to a depth of untouched
darkness,
Where unknown secrets of nature
wait in seeking.

Where animals of beauty are
animals of poison
And the plants sway in the soft blue
current.

Dashing schools of painted fish
An angels version of utter bliss.
This warm, calm place of heaven.

Though secrets of the world below
Are secrets that we'll never know
We will relentlessly explore
The world wide seas from shore to shore.

Catherine Macfarlane (13)
Caister High School

THE OCEAN BLUE

You sail across
The ocean blue,
The sea is calm
Just a ripple or two.

But down below
It is black as night,
Things lurking around
That may give you a fright.

An octopus
Tentacles spread wide,
Ink squirting out
From his inside.

A fearsome shark
With his pointed teeth,
Appears from behind
The coral reef.

Now coming up
From the depths of the sea,
Into clearer waters
By the quay.

There we can see
Boats old and new,
The fishing nets
And fishermen too.

The waves break
On top of themselves,
Onto the beach
Covered in shells.

Victoria Bower (12)
Caister High School

THE SEAL

I'm swimming here in the sea,
With all my friends around me
My head bobs up and then goes down,
We sometimes like to clown around,
The fish they do around us swim,
For dinner we catch them what a sin.

The fisherman they are a threat,
We can get caught up in their nets,
The pain we suffer because of this,
Is because we try to steal their fish,
My pup got badly hurt one day,
He was caught and taken by the RSPCA.

They took him to a safer place,
Where they could mend his injured face,
The nets they cut into him so far,
He will have a lot of horrid scars,
When they had healed enough to see,
They released my baby back to sea.

Some of my friends are kept in captivity,
To do some tricks for the public to see,
They jump through hoops and balance balls,
This is not natural for them at all,
They should be here with us in the sea,
Not trapped there in captivity!

Rachael Hensher-Spencer (13)
Caister High School

SULTRY SEASONS

Spring:
Animals arise from their wintry graves,
Gradually raising delicate heads,
The ice is slipping away like a dream,
As children pack away their snow-covered sleds.

Summer:
As spring turns a blind eye,
Summer is on its way,
The honey bees are being busy,
And tourists gather in attractions to play.

Autumn:
As the crispy crimson leaves are falling,
Sharp, icy rain comes in sheets,
Children go back to studying,
And tiny animals go back to sleep.

Winter:
As robins perch upon the trees,
Flexing their dainty wings,
Inside, Christmas decorations appear,
And we're dreaming of wonderful things.

Kayley Goodman (13)
Caister High School

My Special Friend The Sea!

I'm standing by my friend,
The most important friend of all,
She's all around the world,
She's anything but small!

She speaks to me in whispers,
She laughs with a great roar!
She cries just like a dolphin,
Waving, screeching, more and more!

I'm not her only friend,
She has plenty of others,
An only child like me,
No sisters or brothers.

She understands my thoughts,
She rarely answers back,
She listens to me personally,
All things that we lack.

She's been here since time began,
Seen the sunrise a million times,
Like the world always changing,
Around it she constantly climbs.

Have you guessed who my special friend is?
A friend to the world, yet destroy her do we?
A home, alive, my friend the . . .

Sea!

Danielle Gilby (13)
Caister High School

UNTITLED

The shapes and voices which surround,
crush and penetrate the boundaries.
I feel oneness in my isolation.

The birds can no longer fly
The children are stilled and quieted,
Like puppets they dance, muted.
Can you hear the silence of coldness?
Frosted eyes and chapped; red noses.
Oh how I wish for long summer days,
And the smell of the warm summer air.

I am held in chaos, in rages, in ribbons.

Here, there are no noises,
I cannot help but miss the smiles,
Laughing faces that were never my own.
Our hair is so dull and our skin is so dry.
But still we want to better ourselves,
Still she has me tied up in knots.

Everything is grey and matted now.
My soft exhausted breath,
A final escape before collapsing deep inside myself.

James Harrod (16)
Earlham High School

CHROMATOGRAPHY

Round fishes swim through coloured water
They shine like stars in the night.
Collecting colours in the stream as they swim.

Karl Hodgson (13)
Fred Nicholson School

FRIENDS

A friend is always there.
My friend is happy.
Sometimes my friend is sad.
I can tell secrets to her.

I can tell stories to my friend.
I can share all my toys.
I can write letters.
I can ring my friend up.

My friend is a good friend.
I can invite my friend to tea.
We can play games.
We talk about boys.
She is my friend.
There is no one else.

Zoe Tigue (13)
Fred Nicholson School

NANCY

Nancy seems dishonest.
She is pretty.
She is young.
She loves Bill.
She wants fun.
She gets into danger.
For Oliver on the run.
Poor Nancy!

Tommy Rump (11)
Fred Nicholson School

LADY IN THE STREET

It is a freezing cold day in winter
The lady wears a dark purple dress,
It is made from velvet
It feels warm and furry
She is tall and slim.
She is rich.

It was a freezing cold day in winter.
The lady wears a drab grey dress
It is made from cotton
It is torn and ragged
She is pale and weak
She is poor.

Emma Unthank (10)
Fred Nicholson School

MUSCLES

Muscles tighten and relax,
tighten and relax.
Body moves, body works.
Muscles burning food,
muscles burning energy.
Body sweats.
Muscles tighten and relax,
tighten and relax.
Start to weaken,
ache and sleep.
Heart beats faster,
brain makes you go
jogging.

David Cooper (14)
Fred Nicholson School

FRIENDS

My friends are happy in my home.
I make the dinner.
They sleep in my bedroom.
It is tidy.
They play with my toys.
My sister is my friend.

Serena Robinson (13)
Fred Nicholson School

LEAVING HOME

Off to fight
Getting up tight,
To get what's right,
In a fight,
In the air.
Shooting.
One by one,
Came down like a kite,
On that night.

Thomas Scott (14)
Fred Nicholson School

FRIENDS

Nicola and Ricky had a band.
And hung out at home.
They drank Coca-Cola.
They went to a party at my house.
They helped me to do my work.

Beth-Ann Peachell (13)
Fred Nicholson School

OLIVER TWIST

Oliver was weak
A frightened hungry boy.
A kind home he'd seek
And bring him joy.
He didn't have any money
Never ate bread and honey.
He was sometimes sad - and funny.
I think he was nice
But he paid the price
Of living in the workhouse
With lice and mice.

Lisa Smibert (11)
Fred Nicholson School

LOLLY MOOR

We went to Lolly Moor
to the wet pond in the rainy woods
with my wet net
I caught wet tadpoles
and wet dragonflies
in the wet green wood
on a wet damp day
wet to the insects
and wet to us.

Lisa Leveridge (12)
Fred Nicholson School

BEST FRIENDS

Best friends, best mates
always go round together
Friends always give spellings
They read to you sometimes.

Friends are boring sometimes
but not all the time
They walk and talk
We need their company.

She fights and breaks up
Then we make up again.

She walks and talks
She always does
We always tell each other jokes
We always laugh together about boys.

Helen Briggs (13)
Fred Nicholson School

HOLIDAYS

It is hot and sunny all day long,
People lazing in the sun,
Staring into space,
Nobody cares about a thing in the world,
So they can imagine the scenery,
Looking in the crystal clear waters,
Getting drunk all day,
Playing on the pleasant beaches
In the soaring sun.

Vicky Barrett (15)
Fred Nicholson School

FARAWAY PLACES

I would like to go
to a faraway place

A place where no people
can be seen

A place where you
can do anything you like

A place that is just for me.

Laurie Sheppard (15)
Fred Nicholson School

RED IS

Red is a fire engine with lights all flashing
Red is a car that drives people home
Red is a tomato, juicy and round
Red is a bead, hard, and a circle.

Tommy Coppelstone (9)
Fred Nicholson School

CROCODILE

Open jaws
Eat an arm
It is crunching bones
One day the crocodile had Mrs Walker.

Michael Patrick (12)
Fred Nicholson School

THUNDER

The thunderstorm
was beginning to *thunder*
Loud and *frightening!*
People were *screaming!*
There is a *tornado* out there
Some of the people died in the *storm.*

Benjamin Lane
Fred Nicholson School

A COMPUTER POEM

The computer talks to me
and tells me what to do.
When I turn it on it says
'Let's play a game.'
We have to take turns
and when I beat the computer
the computer says 'Goodbye.'

David Nobbs (12)
Fred Nicholson School

SCHOOL

School school is a hall
hall in a crocodile's jaws
crocodile spat school into the
dragon's mouth called Mrs Walker
threw us into the garbage can
and the dragon said 'Rowell for victory.'
                    Dead.

Paul White (12)
Fred Nicholson School

FOOTBALL

He's good at running fast with the ball
He's good at doing all sorts of skills
He's good at scoring all the goals
He's good at everything
Nathan Wrigglesworth
World class player.
Superstar!

Nathan Wrigglesworth (13)
Fred Nicholson School

TEACHERS

Teachers are bossy boots
Teachers shout at us
Teachers tell us off
Teachers make us work hard
But . . .

Rhys Packer (11)
Fred Nicholson School

THE ENCHANTED GLADE

The tree is calm
Beautiful, peaceful.
Flowers are beautiful.
The place is lovely.
A honeymoon place
For Captain John Smith and Pocahontas.

Jonathon Hood (12)
Fred Nicholson School

POCAHONTAS

The tree was talking
She talked to John Smith
John Smith kissed Pocahontas
They fell in love
The flowers were lovely
Pocahontas was happy
The birds were singing
Everyone was happy.

Wallis McGhee (11)
Fred Nicholson School

BABIES

The babies are nice
Babies cry and wet their nappies
I like babies
love
Jade.

Jade Manners (11)
Fred Nicholson School

INDIAN MAN

The Indian looked at the man
A man looked at the Indian
The Indian killed a man
The man killed an Indian.

Robert Jackson (11)
Fred Nicholson School

FRIENDS

Friends always stick together
through better and worse
no matter what happens
friends always stick together.

Friends always stick together
they talk to you
they share problems
friends always stick together.

Ben Fincham (14)
Fred Nicholson School

FRIENDS

My friends are happy.
My friends are nice.
My friends are kind.
My friends are helpful.
My friends are friendly.

Nicholas Potter (13)
Fred Nicholson School

COCO POPS

Breakfast gives me strength,
Food gives me health,
Sugar gives me energy,
Chocolate gives me taste,
I'm a strong energetic tasty person.

Adrian Marsh (14)
Fred Nicholson School

RAVING BEAT

I walked down the street,
I'm raving to the beat.

People walk and talk down the street,
Talk, talk, talk.

I walked down the street,
I'm raving to the beat.

Taxi, taxi, taxi driving through the street.

I walked down the street,
I'm raving to the beat.

Rushing, rushing through the street,
To meet my friend in a club.

I'm happy in the club dancing to the beat.

Ian Matthews (14)
Fred Nicholson School

CITY JUNGLE

Stuck in the traffic,
I am sitting in my car.
I am getting fed up.
I am dehydrated,
I want to go home
And have my tea.
I am getting furious,
I am getting thirsty.
I need the toilet.
I am hot.

Robert Benefer (14)
Fred Nicholson School

CITY JUNGLE

I was walking down the street
Rap, rap and rap to the beat.

I rap down the city,
And through a place.
The house recharges me,
Rapping to the beat.

Walking through the park
The people come to me.
We start to rap the beat again,
Again, again to the beat.

I was walking, rapping to the beat,
Past two skyscrapers.
I rap to the beat.

The skyscraper comes alive, alive,
They rap, rap and rap to the beat.

William Petley (14)
Fred Nicholson School

CITY JUNGLE

I was walking down the street,
Rapping to the beat,
Rapping so quickly,
Going to the beat.
Standing on the street,
Looking at the street,
Just watching people,
Standing, standing on the street.

John Morgan (14)
Fred Nicholson School

CITY JUNGLE

I walked past the street cars,
Blue and rusty.
I saw headlights sparkling
Through my face.
I saw the sky so dark and grey.
I heard footsteps rumbling down in the town.
People swaying about in the street.
Fireworks band.
They sparkled in the sky.
People walked under my feet.
I felt so dizzy.
I walked around the town,
The rock music made the windows rattle.

Karl Potter (14)
Fred Nicholson School

CITY JUNGLE

The sky is grey,
And the cars are streaming by.
The birds are grey and black.
There are old houses,
Old as the hills.
People steering by,
Choking on the fumes.
As cars go by,
Double-decker buses roaring by,
As tall as the buildings.
People shouting, music loud,
Until the sun rises again.

Martin Herring (14)
Fred Nicholson School

CITY JUNGLE

I walked down the streets
I'm rapping to the beat.
So charge to the beat,
Brush to the streets.

Looking at the people,
Sitting on the pavement,
Drinking, drinking, drinking.

Looking at the people,
Rushing down the street.
Smoking, smoking, smoking.

Looking at the traffic,
Cars rushing by.
Stinking, stinking, stinking.

I walked down the street,
I'm rapping to the beat.

Carl Wrigglesworth (14)
Fred Nicholson School

MANCHESTER UNITED

I've been to see my team.
Manchester United
Manchester United scored . . . 4
Norwich City scored . . . 3
I went home very happy.

Mark Clapham (12)
Fred Nicholson School

CITY JUNGLE

I was walking down the city
I heard cars zooming by.
Zoom zoom they go by.
I heard loud people shouting.
Drinking all the time.
And I heard a street party.
It is hot and sunny.
Light was on.

Andrea Arnold (14)
Fred Nicholson School

HOLIDAYS

I like holidays all the time, especially drinking
lots of wine.

I like watching people playing in the sun,
playing lots of games, having so much fun.

I like eating and drinking when the sun is hot,
I like sleeping and snoozing quite a lot.

Adam Stanford (15)
Fred Nicholson School

THE ENCHANTED GLADE

There were lots of trees
The willow tree can talk
Pocahontas fell in love.

Gemma Raper (11)
Fred Nicholson School

ENGLAND, ENGLAND ARE THE BEST

England, England are the best
They can do anything.
They are the best.
They win football matches.
They are the best in the World Cup.
England are the champs.
One of them lost his football kit at the big match.

Daniel Marsh (11)
Fred Nicholson School

THE CAT

The cat cried.
The cat scratched.
The cat miaowed.
The cat was asleep.

Christine Syer (11)
Fred Nicholson School

POND LIFE

Beside the yellow in green grass flowers
in the tall trees of the wood
I saw an oval tadpole with
a long curved tail
in the cold wet water of the day.

Natalie McQuillan (14)
Fred Nicholson School

I AM ALONE

I'm alone,
I'm on my own,
No one's there,
No one to care,
No one to turn to,
No one to see,
I feel everybody's staring at me,
I know they don't like me,
I know they don't care,
But I wish someone was there,
Someone to talk to,
Someone to tell,
My feelings inside,
To just know them well.

Crystal Crook (13)
Hethersett High School

THE BEAST CALLED HOMEWORK

Sometimes I'm asked to write a poem
I say 'Why?'
What is it you ask of me?
What part of me do you want to plough from?
What part of me do you want to see
thrown across this white piece of paper?
What do I get out of this?
Nothing!
I have to give this to you,
for no more reason than it is the name
of the beast called *homework*.

Matt Musson (14)
Hethersett High School

THE CLOUD ABOVE WITH MY LOVE

I can't help myself, I'm always
in the clouds above thinking of things that I love.
I will never stop thinking of things I love.
I'm still in the clouds above thinking of the person I love.
I think I'm floating down thinking of something
bad
But I'm just above the clouds above.
Now I'm floating up above the clouds thinking
of the one I love.
Now I'm back with the fairies dancing about
in my mind.
'I'm going now' I say, I'm back in my classroom
next to the one I love.
But never mind
I will get back to the clouds above with the fairies
I was dancing with up above in the cloud of love.

Lucy Fincham (13)
Hethersett High School

A SHADOW OF BLACK

Black and white the picture of life,
An endless circle trapped in time,
A lifeless body in a freeze-frame,
The drips from an iceberg splashed in pain,
An empty room with a smiling face,
An enchanted valley versus the starry space,
A world split in two by an invisible line,
As the life from our planet is left behind.

Jennifer Fell (13)
Hethersett High School

I'M FINE THANK YOU!

There is nothing the matter with me,
I'm as healthy as can be.
I have arthritis in both my knees
and when I talk, I talk with a wheeze.
My pulse is weak and my blood is thin,
but I'm awfully well for the shape I'm in.

Arch supports I have for my feet,
or I wouldn't be able to be on the street.
Sleep is denied me night after night,
but every morning I find I'm alright.
My memory is failing, my head's in a spin,
but I'm awfully well for the shape I'm in.

The moral is this as my tale I unfold,
that for you and me who are growing old,
it's better to say 'I'm fine' with a grin
than to let other folks know the shape we are in.

Nathan Barker (12)
Hethersett High School

SEA LIFE

The creatures in the sea,
Are very much like you and me,
Every one of us is different,
From the tiny ant to the enormous elephant.

The creatures in the sea,
Can be as different as you from me.

Laura Crack (12)
Hethersett High School

HUNTED

I saw a pretty sight today,
little fox cubs out to play,
mother fox was very near,
she knew they had no sense of fear.
She guarded them with eagle eye,
she knew the huntsman may pass by.

Then suddenly she heard the sound
of horses' hooves upon the ground.
She called her fox cubs to her side
and fled into the wood to hide.
For she had dug a cosy den
to keep her family safe from men
who have no loving care or thought,
the cruel ones who hunt for sport.

David Bedford (13)
Hethersett High School

THE BEAUTIFUL DOLPHINS

The beautiful dolphins swam around
the wavy swimming pool,
Frantically and nervously trying to do
different tricks.
While the big, boisterous, bullying crowd
were waiting for the show to finish,
as everyone thought it was boring,
as they couldn't do any of the tricks,
because they were still too young.

Laura Barker (14)
Hethersett High School

THE EAGLE

Eagle of the night
Flying high in the sky,
Sent by a spirit
Spirit of an Indian Brave.

Eagle of the night
Flying high in the sky,
Hunting for his prey,
By night and day.

Eagle of the night
Flying high in the sky,
Seeing everything an Indian sees,
With his eagle eye.

Maxine Friend (12)
Hethersett High School

WHAT IS DYING?

A ship sails, and I stand watching, till she fades
on the horizon and someone says 'She is gone!'
Gone where? Gone from my sight, that is all.
She is just as large as when I saw her.
The diminished size and total loss of sight
is in me, not in her, and when someone at my side says
'She is gone,' there are others who are watching her coming
and others who take up the glad shout
'Here she comes.'
And that is dying!

Lucy Churchill (13)
Hethersett High School

A Girl's World

Shopping trips and make-up tips
Are what it's all about.
Boys and hair and nail care
Are what we shout about.

Slamming doors and blocked up pores
Prove to be a pain.
Little sis, her hissy fits,
Can drive a girl insane.

Punching fights and flashing lights
Aren't our kind of scene.
Horror vids and muddy kids
Seem to make us *scream.*

Football cheers and funny peers
Cheer us up no end.
Clothes and bags and fancy mags
We give our friends to lend.

Pumping sounds and dancing crowds
Is where we will be found.
Rap and rock and Indie pop
Is what we play aloud.

Laughs and giggles explain it all,
Bring us close together.
Chats and talks and long phone calls
Seem to last forever.

Lucy Underwood (12)
Hethersett High School

HORSES

The gigantic horse galloping,
The tiny horse trotting,
The new horse neighing,
The shire horse shambling,
The carthorse carting,
The thoroughbred horse tripping,
The champion horse chewing,
The cute horse cantering,
The rampaging horse rolling,
The dainty horse dressage,
The shy horse showing.

Elizabeth Keay (14)
Hethersett High School

THE CLASSROOM

I sat in the classroom looking at my
work,
Thinking, what's it all about?
The teacher was talking, and
drinking coffee,
Like she hadn't got a thought in the
world,
I sat looking at the window, like I
was suddenly dreaming,
The fantasy left my mind.

Emma Forster (13)
Hethersett High School

SPELING

i'm no good at speling
i'm not worryed
the techers all tel me
I nied to lern

how to spel i do not no
i dont care
i will servive with out noing
how to spel

nether do i no
all abote punkshoashon
no full stops nor comers
no exlamashon marks

no qweshton mars
no nothing
not evan capetal leters
just badley spellt words

Katrina Marshall (13)
Hethersett High School

FISHING

Sitting there on the bank
Watching the fish jump out of the water
And the current swirling and clashing against the
shore
And the float bobbing up and down
Like it had the hiccups
And all of a sudden it went under
It looked like it had drowned.

Kelvin Barker (14)
Hethersett High School

THE GOLDFISH

T he goldfish swam
H igh over the hills
E veryone could see it

G ood as gold it was
O ver and under the water it went
L ots of people grabbing it
D on't want to catch it really but I have to
F ish and chips for supper
I sn't that a delight
S uch a mess it made
H urtling around the bank at night

S wirling and crawling around as well
W aiting to catch it
A nd waiting to eat it, yes I ate it at once
M unch, munch. That fish was nice.

Claire Keenan (15)
Hethersett High School

CATS

The tall tabby cats twitching
The beautiful black cats bouncing,
The small scared cats scratching,
The smelling Siamese cats sniffing,
The cute cuddly cats crawling,
The perfect Persian cats purring,
The massive Manx cats miaowing.

Gemma Easter (14)
Hethersett High School

A POEM ABOUT BEING LATE

L ate up
A detention for being late
T eacher tells me off for not doing my homework
E nemies kick me in the head

F our teachers on my back
O ut of the class said Mr Baldwin
R un to lunch

S coff it down my throat
C hair breaks and I get into trouble
H ometime at last
O ut of the kitchen said nasty Dad
O ut of my room said horrible sister
L ate in bed and nasty Dad hit me.

Matthew Kingsley (13)
Hethersett High School

TEENAGER

Life is very confusing,
And I do not know why.
For all the questions I keep asking,
Are answered with only a sigh.

I feel like a walking disaster,
Accidents just seem to appear.
Things always fall on the floor,
Especially when I am near.

The giggles come so easily,
And never seem to end.
When laughing for no reason,
Sends everyone around the bend!

My friends all think I'm 'different'
And I'm inclined to agree.
For no one seems to understand
The difficulties of being me.

Suzie Fickling (13)
Hethersett High School

WONDERED!

Have you ever really wondered what's lurking
behind the door?
Or in the cupboard where no one ever goes?
Or deep in the night you feel a sudden chill and
wonder if it's something really untold?

Have you ever really wondered what's behind
all those green trees?
Or waiting to find out what's hiding in those bushy hedges?
Or what's really lurking in those woods?

Have you ever really wondered what's swimming
in the sea?
Or waiting in the deep end for its mid afternoon tea?
Or where does that sucky thing go when the day is all cool?

Well to tell you the truth
No! I don't wonder.

Shona Gent (13)
Hethersett High School

MY DAD'S DOG

Jock is my dad's dog,
He is a terror,
He eats scraps that we leave
and he annoys dad sometimes,
but mostly he plays
with dad
and me.
When my dad leaves him
he sulks in his office.
Sometimes my dad takes
him in the van
to work.
He likes that.
And at supper time he
mooches for food.
And at night sometimes
I hear him through the wall.
My dad tells him to lie
on his quilt.
sometimes I take him
for walks.
If he's good.
Although he's dad's dog
I love him like
he's mine.

Tom Swanston (13)
Hethersett High School

MY MAGNIFICENT BOX

I will put in my box
The wings of a flying fish,
The whisper of the wind,
One of Pegasus's feathers
And a slice of cloud.

I will put in my box
The smell of sea spray,
The tip of a dragon's tail,
a star all of my own in a little glass box
And a tiny dinosaur.

I will put in my box
The salty tear of a crocodile,
A dove of peace,
The eye of a Cyclops
And a lick of fire from the sun.

I will put in my box
The horn of a unicorn,
An angel's halo
And a bolt of lightning.

My box is made with
A dragon's scale
And coloured glass,
A patch of untouched snow
And happy dreams.

I shall skate in my box
On Saturn's great rings,
Then I shall ride Haley's comet
Rushing at light speed
Through space.

Anna Percy-Burns (12)
Hewett School

SUGARCOAT

I was seven when she joined our class.
Her name was Sonia. She didn't speak much English.
They said she was from Russia.
They showed us on the map.
   It was pink.

They said a bad thing happened there
When Sonia and us were only babies.
They said that was why Sonia
Sometimes was sick, why her hair kept coming out.
They said
   That they gave her magic medicine.

She had a lot of fun.
They took her to Pleasurewood Hills,
To Alton Towers.
She had a ride in a hot air balloon.
We didn't see why we
Couldn't ride in a hot air balloon.

Then one day
She never came to school anymore.
They said there had been
Something very wrong
In her head.

When I got older
I wondered what the bad thing in Russia was.
   I found out
      And then I cried.

Sarah Peploe (12)
Hewett School

MY MAGICAL BOX

I will put in my magical box
the touch of a tiny twinkling twilight star,
a pack of ponies prancing across the plains of America
and the sun's heated rays raining down upon my back.

I will put in my magnificent box
the nuzzling neck of a velvet tiger,
the steep climb of a high mountain
and the glistening water of wonderful Lake Windermere.

My magical box is the haunt of
a dolphin's dainty calm cry,
a never-ending silence only broken by the whistle of the wind
and the long-lasting laugh of a hyena.

My magical box is home to
a pod of whales swimming silently through a summer sky,
a fluffy cloud floating upon the Pacific ocean
and a moonless eclipse of dreams.

My magical box is composed of hundreds of stars
intricately entwined with fuchsia-coloured flowers.
When opening the box the air is filled with birds singing
and the sweet aroma of jasmine.

I will then waltz in my box
across the wild west of Texas,
then dance across Oklahoma and Colorado
to the green grass of Wyoming.

Angie Childerhouse (12)
Hewett School

WISHERS

When wishing, when wishing, when wishing for what you want,
you never give up from day to day, night to night,
month to month, year to year.
When you find your king, or your queen, or even your hero,
don't give up, hang in there,
you never know what might be round the corner.
When wishing, when wishing, when wishing for what you want,
and no hope, keep hope.
Hope is a thing like a bird on the wing flying away,
journey to journey, journey to journey,
and that bird keeps hope because it needs to fly,
like a cow has to have milk and a dog has to bark.
When wishing, when wishing, when wishing for what you want,
don't give up and forget everything like it's never happened, try.
Life goes on and we do not know what lies ahead for us.
That's why we must work and sacrifice things
because the scientists work well with chemicals,
and lorry drivers work well with trucks,
and the electricians work well with electricity.
But if we all wish for peace and happiness, we will all live happily.
When wishing, when wishing, when wishing for what you want,
keep your dreams and they will come true.

Johnny Stokes (13)
Langley School

SPIDERS

Up the wall and in you crept,
With your light-footed steps,
Scampering across the kitchen floor,
With your eight legs on the door,
Under you squeezed hoofing and poofing,
Not knowing your fatal death.

Walking along happily,
Then you hear a sudden shriek,
'Kill it' you hear but not knowing the meaning,
You felt a light earthquake
That gave you a sudden fright,
But it got heavier and louder,
Until there was only a *big shoe in sight!*

Christabelle Macfoy (12)
Langley School

SUMMER V WINTER

Summer can be blissful
Although it can be dull
The golden sun is shining
The bees have started stinging
The beach is very lovely
But not with busy pink bodies
The sea is cool and blue
Infested with jellyfish chasing after you.

Oh why can't it be winter?
It is all the same to me
The tiny flakes of gentle snow
Fall slowly to the ground
The cruel wind blowing crisp leaves gently to the earth
The children skate across the sparkling icy pond
The cobwebs glisten in the morning dew
But of course the best of all is Christmas time
Which is loved by me and you.

Sarah Wharton (13)
Langley School

CARS

Cars, cars most excellent cars
My whole life revolves around them,
From the noise that they make to the speed they undertake,
It's the most fantastic thing there could be,
From Ladas to Ferraris, Skodas to Dodge Vipers
It's enough to make me want to drool,
From 1 litre to 8 litre, anything will do,
It's most everything that will interest me,
Just tell me the spec and I will freeze in sheer excitement,
Next thing I'll want a test drive,
Then I'll say 'How much do you want for it?'
And if you say 'No sale'
I'll be gone like a flash, chasing the next car owner.

Daniel King (12)
Langley School

WINTER'S MESSAGE

Wet and windy, dull and bleak,
In the winter there is no peace
Nothing stops the blistering rage.
The thunder, the lightning
The eternal rain.
The winter's bold,
The winter's cold.
The ice is set,
And the ground is wet.
Winter is to stay,
And to make us pay!

Emma Tills (12)
Langley School

CHRISTMAS

Christmas presents, little treats,
Sitting under Christmas trees.
Christmas puddings, large stuffed turkeys,
Waiting on the table.
Big bright stars, little sweets,
Hanging on the Christmas tree.
Christmas crackers, small surprises,
Waiting to be revealed.
Trees and houses, lawns and bushes,
Covered white with snow.
One large carrot, a glass of wine,
Lying near the fireplace.
Across the sky, on the roof,
Scuttling down the chimney.
What is it? Where's it from?
Why is it in the chimney?
A big bird? A burglar?
I have no idea.
Out come legs, now a tummy,
And a big brown sack.
I know now, who it is,
It is Santa Claus.
Out come presents, big and small,
Then he drinks his wine.
Takes the carrot, up the chimney,
And off into the Christmas night.

Fiona How (12)
Langley School

PLAY SOLDIERS

CCF, CCF it's the thing I most detest.
Marching up, marching down, a very boring fest.
Uncomfortable the clothes may be, and stylish they are not.
The malignant blisters need not be forgot.

But now there's a promise of an RAF section.
The army will suffer from severe rejection.
Mr Gardner with his hopes of flight.
Leaving Mr Morgan with hate and spite.

But by the time this section goes ahead,
The majority of us will be dead.
I would not mind a look at it though
Perhaps if they're lucky, I will give it a go.

James Greengrass (13)
Langley School

MY LONELY BAMBI

Standing in a lonely stable
I wait all alone there's no one to care now
as my charges have grown and gone.
We all loved our days in the sunshine
as we cantered through the meadow.
Now no one comes to ride me
and my days are empty and long.
I'm grey and my bones are showing,
but I'm still hoping for some child to visit me
and say 'Come on let's go'.
The days of fun we shared
will remain with me forever.

Abbie Roper (12)
Langley School

GLUTTONY

Food is wonderful,
Food is great;
Never for a meal,
Am I late!

Wasting lots of food,
On vast food mountains;
As well as wine and milk lakes,
They must have food fountains.

Throwing all that food away,
In that big, black bin;
When people are starving in the world,
Surely this must be a sin.

Darren Gee (13)
Langley School

RUGBY

R ugby's a sport for hard nuts.
U nified men in suits.
G uys with bodies of steel.
B oys with brains and passion for the game.
Y oung ladies can play and go quite far.

T he England Team perhaps.
E veryone is able to play.
A s long as you're in top condition.
M aybe you'll get into the team.
S o if you want to have a go,
    take a shot and have some fun.

Richard J Hutchins (12)
Langley School

WIND

Wind takes our thoughts around the world.
It whispers them to everyone.
You can hear them as the wind whispers them to everything it passes,
Have you heard . . .
Did you know . . .
Did you hear about . . .
I never realised.
All of my secrets,
All of my wishes, my dreams, my hates and my loves.
They're not mine anymore.
The whole world knows them.
But everyone is too busy to stop and realise,
to pause,
to listen,
to notice what the wind is whispering.
Except maybe someone who has stopped just long enough,
to hear what the wind is saying.
That person knows my thoughts.
But did you ever stop to think,
It knows yours too?

Frances Cockerill (12)
Langley School

BOREDOM

As my pen touches my paper
My brain swells,
My mind explodes,
My imagination wanders.

I lean on my desk,
Searching for something I cannot find,
I open my eyes . . .
and it's right in front of me.

I don't know what it is
But it's there.
I can't see it,
I can't touch it,
But I know it's there.

As I glance at my watch
and think 'How much longer'?
The bell rings.

As I step outside,
It hits me.
I knew what that was,
What I couldn't see,
What I couldn't feel,
What was there all along . . .
Boredom . . .

Harriet Rayne (13)
Langley School

THE BEACH

The sea's
Crashing, thunderous roar
Deafening to those who hear.
Going out
Coming in like the seasons
Of a year.

The spiteful
Howling, chilling wind
Sweeping down the beach.
Shooting here
Moving there, making sounds
Pleasing to hear.

Oliver Tills (13)
Langley School

THE HOSPITAL

I hate the injections, the needles are so sharp
I think I am going to bleed
I hate the blood
It's like lava coming out of a volcano
I hate the screams, so shrill
I think the screaming person could be me!
I hate the way the doctors stare
As if I am next on their plate for lunch
Hospitals - why do they fill me with fear?

Thomas Lardner (12)
Langley School

SUICIDAL

In the darkness
there is only one
light.
'What light?'
you say,
'What light?'

In his mind
there is only one
thought.
'What thought?'
you say,
'What thought?'

In his heart
there is only one
passion.
'What passion?'
you say,
'What passion?'

In his conscience
there is only one
doubt.
'What doubt?'
you say,
'What doubt?'

Joseph Hodgkin (13)
Langley School

FOOD

Food here, food there,
Don't you find it so boring?
Yet people love it.
Food, food, food

You see it at home,
You see it at school.
Yes, people need it
Food, food, so much of it

Food couldn't be addictive
You see people that could call it dangerous
They're addicted to it.
Food, food, food

The countries of starvation
You see them on the television.
Now those are the people that wish for a miracle
Yet they get so little of it

Food here, food there
Think how lucky we are.
So always remember those countries out there.

Sam Grimsdell (12)
Langley School

GOLF

Golf is wonderful,
Golf is great,
Putting on that green,
You have got to concentrate.

Going on the driving range,
Oh what fun,
I jumped for joy with happiness,
When I bagged my first hole in one.

Teeing off
Towards the hole in the woods,
Putting for birdie,
It feels good.

Playing at school,
Or my local club,
I always seem to lose my ball,
In that pest of a shrub.

Golf is wonderful,
Golf is great,
Teeing off on that first hole,
You have got to concentrate.

Oliver Hewkin (13)
Langley School

THE CHARGE OF THE TIGHT BRIGADE

The noble men were ordered
Into doing something wrong,
They were ordered to charge right into
A blaring, flashing throng.

The six hundred had no chance,
As they were duly pelted,
There was no way they would survive,
Even if they had been sheltered.

Red blotches made them redder
Than their clothes already were,
The thought of just retreating,
To them did not occur.

One by one the six hundred fell,
They were quite overpowered,
By the superior foe they fought,
By whom they were being showered.

The tomatoes were starting to hurt them
As the men scattered everywhere,
The audience with their rotten fruit,
Gave each dancer his fair share.

The male ballet dancers
With their show lying in tatters,
Realised that keeping the show ongoing
Is not the only thing that matters.

The men in tights retreated
With their tights a-laddering,
From that day on the six hundred men,
Stuck to gardening.

Paul Nahai Williamson (13)
Langley School

CAIRO

Cairo the bustling city
The city which has no pity
The city which is not gooey
And has little duty

The leaning tower of Pisa
Is not as nice as the pyramids of Giza
And the mighty sphinx
Just as beautiful as minx

The amazing Cairo tower
So full of power
Where it stands on an isle
On the Nile

Just like a sweet dove
And so full of love
As it flows through the city
So peaceful and witty

The gift of the Nile
Without it the land would be vile
With beautiful and impressive mosques
Down to the ticket kiosks

The mighty solid gold mask of Tutankhamun
Is just waiting for you to come in
The Valley of the Kings
Is just full of old things

Five thousand years ago a pharaoh ruled
And now he is overruled
Now it is a Republic
So think the public.

Karim Molyneux-Berry (13)
Langley School

THE TEACHER FROM HELL

Walking through those dreaded doors,
Not knowing where she's lurking.
She'll eat you up with her bloodsucking jaws,
She'll tear you down with her three-inch claws.
That's the teacher from hell, behind those doors.

You'll be scared and you will be frightened,
Her face couldn't ever be lightened.
Inside the four walls of that room,
Say your prayers, for you're going to meet your doom.
That's the teacher from hell, behind those doors.

Beware beware beware I say,
Are you ready to meet your doomsday?
She breathes fire, she breathes smoke,
She'll smoke you till you choke.
That's the teacher from hell, behind those doors.

I once before saw a young boy die,
For he perhaps told a lie.
She is mean, she is ugly,
That's the teacher from hell, behind those doors.

Samuel Healy (13)
Langley School

LADY

As I sit here watching her
I realise how lucky I am.
I look at her sparkling mane and tail,
Swishing the flies off her gleaming body.
She has no worries.
She takes mouthfuls of grass,
She leaps up and down,
And trots back and forth,
In her dew-covered field.
As I reach the fence she canters to greet me,
Placing her cool velvety nose in my palm.
As I stroke the side of her smooth shimmering face
She closes her eyes,
As if trusting me completely.
She whinnies softly
As if saying goodbye,
Then trots back up the hill,
And carries on eating her lush grass,
Not a care in the world.

Kate Jones (13)
Langley School

MADEIRA

Bread, break, the sea breaks on the ship's side,
Blow, blow, the wind blows the salt up from the sea,
And the passengers, in this rough weather,
Retire to their cabins queasy and off-colour,
The crew although nauseated, stays up on deck and labours,
The sight of queasy passengers, not rousing them from work.

Break, break, the sea breaks upon Madeira's shore,
Blow, blow, the wind blows up in the mountains far,
And the passengers in their wicker sledges,
Scream with fright and delight as they whizz round the corner,
The crew, although fast, get weary feet quickly,
And even when their hats blow off, they get moving again briskly.

Break, break, the sea breaks on the ship's side,
Blow, blow, the wind blows the salt up from the sea,
And the passengers, they stagger to their cabins again,
As they become nauseated and off-colour again,
The crew, although sick of this sight,
Keep working, late into the night.

Andrew Macardle (13)
Langley School

LIGHT AFTER DEATH

There was a silence that compelled no light
The coffin lay watched until it was moved out of sight.
He would watch no more sunsets
He would no more see the birds and the blue sky
His friends will think of how they met him
And how to move on through the silence again and again
they must try.

A child weeps as if forever
The man lies in that box, can't wake up, never.
Outside the day is warm and the sun shines,
Inside there is just darkness, deep darkness
Which reaches the heart of every person as if entwined
By a magical force, no more, no less.

And yet when the doors opened and light came in bit by bit,
A ray of disentangled hope, though unknown came with it.
People's hearts would soon warm again
Because life will go on if there's hope.
Even though after death nothing is the same
Silence will go, and light shall come back and they will cope.

Nelly Hipkin (13)
Langley School

FOOTBALL DREAMS

On Sunday morning we drove to the pitch,
And I saw an abandoned car in the ditch.
I got to the changing rooms and put on my kit,
Oh why did I pick the one that didn't fit.
I fastened my new, brilliant boots,
They set me back quite a bit of loot.

The lads and I went off for a warm-up,
I really wanted to win the League Cup.
We took our positions to start the match,
Our keeper is good, all the shots he should catch.
The whistle blew, I was very excited,
By my mum and dad, I was being sighted.

We started off at a steady pace,
Although I got hit in the face.
We went one-nil down; I was quite upset,
Until my friend put one in the back of the net.
When half-time came, I didn't want to play much more.
But I had a drink and I was ready for war.

In the second half the crowd was roaring,
And inside my spirit was soaring.
The match was over the cup was won,
We went off cheering, the day was done.
The season is over, the players can rest.
I hope next year we're still the best.

James Raywood (13)
Langley School

THEY WERE THE MEN WITH THE GUN

She ran through the woods,
And out to the road.
She could hear them behind,
Puffing with their load.
       They were the men who were after her,
       They were the men with the gun.

Along the empty street,
And into the park.
Followed her they did,
Even in the dark.
       They were the men who were after her,
       They were the men with the gun.

Through the streets she ran,
Into the dusky night.
She could not see them,
Now there was no light.
       They were the men who were after her,
       They were the men with the gun.

Katharine Thistlethwayte (13)
Langley School

GHOSTS

G rim they are,
H air standing up,
O pen that door to get a
S care from
T hose horrible ghouls. They are bad
S o stay away!

Aaron Fiorentini (12)
Lynn Grove GM High School

THE TITANIC

They said it would never sink,
But who can tell, until a tragedy happens,
It takes just a blink,
A single moment in time.

'Iceberg ahead!' cried the watchmen,
The captain spluttered in his tea,
he ran to the bridge at fast pace,
Most desperately.

The Titanic was steered left,
Scraping the iceberg which had threatened them,
Glad to see the back of it,
They all gave a sigh of relief hoping it would never happen again.

A hole was produced in the side of the ship,
Much to the crew's dismay,
for the ship they said would never sink,
Was doing so that very day.

When the alarm was sounded,
People panicked, children cried,
The men tried to take control,
But feared for their lives.

The captain ordered women and children first,
Last of all him,
he was going down with the Titanic,
To leave now would be a sin.

Rush to the lifeboats,
Splash into the sea,
Every man, woman and child,
Asking 'Why me?'

There were not enough lifeboats for everyone,
Those who could not get on would die,
The boats were almost full, but still more people,
Why not put more lifeboats on, oh why?

The lifeboats were overcrowded now,
People were jumping overboard everywhere,
The boat was sinking fast,
The thought of dying and leaving his wife was
something he could not bear.

The captain retreated to his cabin,
With several tears in his eyes,
he took one last look at the family portrait,
And uttered a final goodbye.

Matthew Lewis, Lee Pettingill & Adrian Smith (13)
Lynn Grove GM High School

THE CREATURE'S PROWLING PRIDE

You can't run, you can't hide,
From this creature's prowling pride,
It sleeps by day,
And hunts by night,
If you should see it *what a fright!*
So if you're out alone *beware!*
You never know who's hiding out there,
On the moors or in the streets,
This creature's looking for some meat,
Prepare yourself for the worst,
'Cos he could be dying from hunger and thirst,
Until he's caught, let's run and hide,
But remember you can't escape from his prowling pride.

Melanie Brinded (13)
Lynn Grove GM High School

BEASTLY POEMS

The beast of Harveston moors
he has definitely been here before
Chunder's hens
were quiet in the pen
When the beast sneaked up and attacked.

The beast of Harveston moors
he has definitely been here before
Poor old Ned
Had to walk in the shed.
To collect all the dead hens.

The beast of Harveston moors
he has definitely been here before
Sad old Bill
felt really quite ill
When he saw all the cherished hens.

Matthew Bexfield (13)
Lynn Grove GM High School

MY FRIEND

R yan is my friend, he is as
Y oung as me,
A little
N oise will disturb him.

S ometimes he's
C lever, he is an
O rdinary boy who has a lot of
T ime, he is also a
T errifying boy!

David Lepage (12)
Lynn Grove GM High School

A RECIPE FOR A COOL KID

Take one spot-infested, ordinary teenager and pour into bathroom.
Add hot water and shower head to rinse clean.
Take out, dry thoroughly and dust lightly with talc.
Now spray all over with designer cologne.
Begin to dress with rugged jeans and brown leather belt.
Add half a tub of grease to hair and slick back carefully.
Then finish dressing with plaid shirt and add more cologne.
Apply with special care to under the arms.
Now pour back into bedroom.
Mix with money, shoes and classy jacket.
Then send out into world to cool with mates.

Charlotte Knight (13)
Lynn Grove GM High School

A TRICK OF THE LIGHT

I saw a man who wasn't there,
Crouching down with long, white hair,
A coat of brown and boots of red,
A golden crown upon his head.
A carpet of leaves, all gold and new,
Covered in the morning dew.
Broken twigs and conker shells,
Mushrooms and toadstools nod like bells.
He starts to dance in the swirling breeze,
And sings his song in tune with the trees.
He disappears into the wood,
I'd follow him if I thought I could!

Emily Harrison (12)
Lynn Grove GM High School

GROWING

Crying, screaming, shouting, it's all happening at once,
It used to be so calm before but now we've come to the crunch.
The start of a living nightmare to be,
A baby has been born you see!
It's all going smoothly deep in their hearts,
But wait until it's two, then it will start!
Furniture ruined, food fights every night,
The whole thing's turning into a terrible fright.
Once they get through their third year rage.
You get to a slightly better stage.
Quieter, more human, the 'School Effect'
Amazed at what they've learnt I expect.
Now we come to the stress phase,
Homework, homework, the teachers' craze.
You always get too much, not enough hours in the day,
Soon the holidays will be here, *whey hey!*
Responsibility is coming, adulthood is here,
Soon comes your worst fear,
Old age!

Zoe Mellor (12)
Lynn Grove GM High School

THE BIG, BAD BEAST

The big, bad beast of Harveston moors
Sneaked up through the allotment doors
The chickens fled as the beast was fed
And the beast had bloody paws.

Bad news for Stone Cross Mill
As the beast headed towards Bill
Chunder was upset and beaten
His chickens had been eaten
This beast was soon to kill.

Keith Paler (13)
Lynn Grove GM High School

SNOWDROP

I sit here alone, untouched by hate and anger.
Alone under my tree with the spiders and the woodlice.
Alone with the stones and the earth.
Alone . . . alone . . . alone.
I am the first of many, the first of beauty.
I am the first of my kind, the first to arrive on this
                                        snow-scattered morning.
I sit here alone waiting for my brothers and sisters.
Will they come . . . will they come . . .
Am I to be the only one.
To see the world this year.
Or will they come . . .
I sit here alone.
Alone . . . alone . . . alone . . .
I am the first to come.
I am the first of many.
I wait for my brothers and sisters.
Will they come . . . will they come . . . will they come . . .
I hope that they come . . . I hope that they come.
I don't want to be alone.

Charlotte Walters (12)
Lynn Grove GM High School

WHEN I AM OLD I WILL

When I am old I will
Race down the sea front,
Drink coke not tea,
Pinch grapes in Tesco.

When I am old I will eat McDonalds and KFC every night,
I will wear the latest fashions,
And go to every nudist beach in the world.

When I am old I will go on scary rides at theme parks,
I will get up at 12 noon,
And go to nightclubs every night.

When I am old I will go to bed at 3am.

Robert Harwood (13)
Lynn Grove GM High School

THE DEVIL'S BEAST

There once was a beast who prowled the moors
Who like to feast on chickens.

His claws were long, and his teeth were sharp,
And he used them to rip up his victims.

With feathers hanging from his mouth,
And blood dripping from his claws,

This beast that was sent by the devil
Keeps on prowling the moors.

Michael Balls (13)
Lynn Grove GM High School

THE BEAST

The beast is near,
Its prodigious claws, its colossal jaws.
It's coming,
You know it's coming,
Do you run or do you hide?
Either way you know it's here, prowling about.
The beast is formidable,
You are ineffectual to it.
Standing there paralysed, thinking
What should I do?
Where should I go?
As the beast is advancing on you.
Still, you stand there, paralysed, thinking
Will I get caught?
Will I survive?
Frantically charging, the beast is closing in.
Every second the situation is getting more intense,
More savage and more wild.
You start running, but the beast gains.
Your mind is frozen in terror.
The beast is rigorously trying to catch and exterminate you.
You run, you run as hard as you can,
But it doesn't get you anywhere.
It's here,
You know it's here.
In the frenzied struggle you run,
It maliciously claws at your leg.
You fall to the ground, your time has expired and your last seconds
Fade away as you enter oblivion from his final thrusting claw.

Michael Gricks (13)
Lynn Grove GM High School

MOTHER'S LOVE

I really, really love my mum,
She must think cleaning's really fun.
She cleans until no dust is found,
As if the Queen is coming round.

When Sunday comes she makes a roast,
With chickens from the nearby coast.
For afters we have chocolate cake,
Which takes ages for her to make.

Late at night it's time for bed,
I hear it ringing in my head.
Mum and dad stay down stairs to watch,
Really sad movies on the box.

I speak for children near and far,
If they're at home or in a car.
To all mums in every way,
Have a happy Mother's Day.

Claire Bishop (13)
Lynn Grove GM High School

THE BEAST OF HARVESTON

There is a beast of Harveston
So everybody says,
It could be big,
It could be small,
It could be round,
It could be tall,
But most of all it has a lust,
For guts and gore.
So take care, it could still be out there.

Tim Weller (13)
Lynn Grove GM High School

GETTING OLD

It was a dark night, the mist had rolled in from the sea,
Susan was walking alone down Avon Green.
She could hear the trees rustling.
The air was moist and damp,
She could hear the creaking of the gate in the distance.
All of a sudden she did feel alone. She could hear footsteps.
Where were they? She didn't know.
She started to quickly walk, so do the footsteps.
She could see a group of people at the bus stop.
Instantly she thought safety, but then a hand grabbed her coat.
She tries to run, faster but can not. She trips over into a puddle.
She can hear heavy breathing above her left shoulder.

Cathy Norton (13)
Lynn Grove GM High School

THE BEAST

It travels around at night
Killing everything in sight.
Slashing its prey
Then running away
Waiting for another day.

Holding its victim tight
Strong, full of might
Waiting around
Hearing no sound.
The beast is waiting to bite.

Hazel Gray-Read (13)
Lynn Grove GM High School

ALL I WANT IS A FRIEND

Why won't you talk to me?
What have I done?
I sit here alone,
Having no fun.
You laugh at me and call me names,
Why do you play these cruel games?
All I wanted was to be your friend,
Will this pain ever end?
Being alone makes me sad,
What did I do that was so bad?
I like to have fun just like you,
To smile, to laugh, and enjoy myself too.
You do not see the tears I cry,
You do not hear my words, 'I want to die,'
Please see what is happening to me,
Because you are making my life a misery.
Please will you give me just a chance,
Not look past me with half a glance.
All I want is to be your friend,
And for my broken heart to mend.

Jodie McMahon (12)
Lynn Grove GM High School

THE TALE OF THE BEAST

A killer of an animal,
I wonder if he is a cannibal,
Hen, men I wonder who's the next ten,
The king of the crawlers and a king of the moor,
If only that beast was not like before.

Chris James (13)
Lynn Grove GM High School

LOVE IS . . .

Love is pink,
You know like a really nice pen ink.
It tastes like your favourite ice-cream,
Like a happy, happy dream.

Love smells like flowers,
With electric powers.
It looks like white, fluffy clouds,
Like happy people all in crowds.

Love sounds like 'Boyzone',
Like a wedding dress that's not on loan.
It feels like silk,
Like a glass of fresh milk.

Sammie Stygall (13)
Lynn Grove GM High School

IT!

Piercing, humungous green eyes which gleam inside you.
The claws of a demon, like a towering, grizzly bear.
The roar of a lion, so loud and fierce.
The odour of *It* is like unbearable old trainers.
It is 6 feet tall, bigger than me,
I wouldn't want to bump into it in the street.
It has brown, long, thin fur, all wavy and not neat.
White, long fangs, all sharp with bloodstains on them.
It breathes really heavy on your neck.

Samantha Dingle (13)
Lynn Grove GM High School

THE BEAST POEM

The monster of the moors.
The beast with ten great claws.
It crawls and crawls over heath and eats its prey with razor teeth.
It attacks swiftly and with speed and eats as much as one needs.
It climbs here and it climbs there, scaring anything in its path.

The monster of the moors.
The appetite of a giant.
The size of an elephant.
Its paws, as big as dinner plates.
Its mouth, as huge as a football.

The monster of the moors.
The beast with ten great claws.
Will it ever be found?

Stephanie Allen (13)
Lynn Grove GM High School

GROOVY GRANNY

When I am old I will go clubbing in Ibiza
and have big parties.
I will have straight hair and decent clothes,
I will get my nose and belly button pierced.
I will wear make-up and listen to groovy music,
I will drink alcohol,
and I will drink fizzy drinks,
I'm not going to complain about loud music,
I will listen to music full blast.
I will have a big house,
I will be a groovy granny.

Rebecca Rump-Smith (13)
Lynn Grove GM High School

LUNCH BREAK

The dull, grey sky,
The drizzle in the air
A calling from seagulls
And the cold, cold wind.
In the canteen
There is the presence of silence
Occasional shouts from cooks
As the meals are prepared.

Ding, dong, ding!
The bell sounds loud
Children come, forming a crowd.
Chink, chink, chink! Goes vending machines.
Crunch, munch, splurch! Go children well pleased.
Friendly exchanges of a school story,
Hopefully nothing gory!
As the second bell sounds, the children file out
Quite a big rush and a large shout.
The cleaners move in to clean up the mess,
What great gals, good for them! Bless!
As everyone leaves the silence comes back
And all that is heard is the wind.

Ashley Curtis (12)
Lynn Grove GM High School

HAVESTON BEAST POEM!

The Haveston beast, lurking and prowling around,
going up and down the streets.
He is always looking for things to rip to shreds
to take back to his cave.
He is very mischievous and sneaky.

Darryl Clarke (13)
Lynn Grove GM High School

FRIENDS

As I walk onto the stone courtyard, nervous
and scared.
Tagging behind my brother, I looked
around and there she was,
The person I was looking for . . .
my best friend!
Soon to be one of many,
Little did I know that she would find new friends,
that she would move on.

'Never mind' Mum said, 'you'll soon find new
friends.'
'But how, I don't know how,' I say to myself.
'How do you make friends?
I've never done this before.'

Usually you're coached in a classroom
and the teachers make friends for you.
Not anymore 'You're a big girl now' as
they say.

Once more that time has been and gone,
You've taken that step once again.
You've gone up again, you're a big girl again.
Your new school, new teachers . . .
New friends!

Leah Hartwell (12)
Lynn Grove GM High School

WINTER

W hite snow covers the ground
I   n an endless blanket.
N ever-ending life lay there as
T he tiny animals hibernate.
E very hint of light is pigmented with colour,
R eds from the berries and greens from leaves.

Sarah Hardwick (13)
Lynn Grove GM High School

THE INDIAN

Golden feathers
Carefully crafted bow
Ready for battle
With a glimmering axe
No cowboys!

Ben Timewell (12)
Lynn Grove GM High School

PEACH

Perfect and plump,
Soft and furry,
Squashy and sticky,
Luscious and lovely,
Scrumptious and sweet.

A treat to eat!

Jennifer Anne Stacey (13)
Lynn Grove GM High School

RUN

They're off!
Italy taking a fine bend,
Japan on the inside, coming
down the straight,
England, they're in the lead,
What! China! China won!

Jennifer Coward (12)
Lynn Grove GM High School

A MODEL

A model is multicoloured
She is summer.
On a catwalk.
She is the sun.
She is designer clothes.
A long sofa.
A posh clothes show.
A silky peach.

James Mason (13)
Lynn Grove GM High School

ANGER

Anger, black as night,
Comes as fast as a thunderbolt.
Smells like thick decaying smoke,
Tastes as sour as a rotting, mouldy apple.
Sounds like a bomb in full motion,
Anger feels as rough as a big wire brush.

Rebecca Mileham (12)
Lynn Grove GM High School

THE ICE SKATER

Warm socks
Woolly hats
Tense and ready
Getting steady

No ice!

Andrew Heath (12)
Lynn Grove GM High School

SPRINTER

Stretching at the start line,
Ready to run,
Raring to start
Let's go, let's go
Missed the gun!

Glenn Coston (12)
Lynn Grove GM High School

CARS

Shiny and spotless,
Enormous, powerful engine,
Very comfortable seats,
All ready to go,

No petrol!

Joe Hender
Lynn Grove GM High School

WHEN I GET OLD

When I am old I will pinch Tesco's food,
I will eat lots of chocolate,
I will never ever drink tea,
I will shop in Asda every week,
I will wear normal clothes,
I will go nightclubbing every night,
When I am old I will drink coke and Pepsi,
I will stay out till 3 or 4 in the morning,
I will watch cartoons all day long,
When I am old I will play video games.

Kira Talbot (13)
Lynn Grove GM High School

ANGER

Anger is a wicked thing
Devilish red glares down on me
The weather suddenly changes
From spring fresh air
To choking, black fog
Go away ignorant people.
I'm seeing the cloud blow over
I'm balanced between the two
Whatever shall I do?
A beam of light comes shining through
        Anger has gone!

Oliver Burrage (12)
Lynn Grove GM High School

DEPRESSION

Depression is grey,
It tastes of mouldy cheese
and smells like rotten eggs,
It's an endless black tube,
nails scratching down a chalk board,
It makes you feel as if you
have a black cloud hanging over
your head.

Amy Simmons (13)
Lynn Grove GM High School

A BUTLER

A butler is brown.
He is the winter,
In a mansion.
He is stormy.
A butler is a tuxedo,
A really big cadillac.
He is a boring news bulletin,
A stiff chicken leg.

Dominic Gilham (13)
Lynn Grove GM High School

APPLES

Rosy-red,
Deliciously delightful,
Tangy taste,
A treat to eat.

Lauren Emmerson (12)
Lynn Grove GM High School

HOCKEY

Coming up to the goal
Other players chasing
Nets in sight
Here it comes
He shoots

No goal!

Danielle Stanley (12)
Lynn Grove GM High School

APPLES

Hard and crunchy
Bitter and sweet,
Green and tasty
Great to eat.

Danielle Coulam (12)
Lynn Grove GM High School

PLUM

Round and plump
Sour or sweet
Purple and perfect
Scrumptious to eat.

Jenny Weeks (13)
Lynn Grove GM High School

DINING SIDE

Smells of food whooshing about
every time you move you can smell it more
as the vending machines hum, you dream of hot meals sitting
in front of you, not long from now peace will die
and is replaced by a buzzing kerfuffle. The birds are singing
so I follow their song
they lead me outside where something is wrong,
the wind is blowing, the rain sets in,
the bad weather is here
let it begin.
Hurricane Lynn is on her way, everyone worries, no one will stay.
But I just stand and wait for it to end. Have I gone completely
round the bend?
I listen, I see, I run into the buzzing kerfuffle.
Where the kerfuffle dies and all is lost.
It is replaced by the sweeps of brooms and the crunch of packets
and the smell of death.
it's over, it's ended.
Until tomorrow.

Peter Scrivener (13)
Lynn Grove GM High School

GIRLS

Shining frocks,
Girls in blue.
Come and save me from being kissed,
Oh! Not you!

Lee Ives (12)
Lynn Grove GM High School

THE ASTRONAUT

An astronaut is white,
He is summery,
In his space world,
He is starry,
He is a bulging suit,
A plane with wings,
He is a fantasy show,
A tough bit of beef.

Dane Whiteley (12)
Lynn Grove GM High School

FIREMAN

Yellow and black
He is like the summer sun
Saving lives
Fire engine zooming around,
Like he owns the land
Just a quick ring on the phone
Quick as flame
There when needed
He is a fireman

Tom Clarke (12)
Lynn Grove GM High School

CLOUDS

Figures in the sky,
Balancing on mountain tops
Must be very high.

Lee Caton (12)
Lynn Grove GM High School

POLICEMAN

A policeman is blue,
Dull as the autumn,
In his shiny, fast car,
Dripping with rain,
Wearing a bulging suit,
Filled with weapons,
As hot as a cooker.
Warning all children,
An anti-smoker.

Luke Jackson (12)
Lynn Grove GM High School

THE STUNTMAN

The crash mat is set.
How much money will I get?
I had to fly.
I touched the sky.

I missed the mat
My head went *splat!*

Ryan Twaits (12)
Lynn Grove GM High School

RUGBY

R ough fighting for the ball
U nderneath people that are tall
G oing in for the tackle
B usting ribs makes you crackle
Y es a win for us all.

Greg Ford (12)
Lynn Grove GM High School

WHAT I THINK, FEEL AND SEE

As I sit here in this room,
I sit and think all alone,
In 30 minutes there will be . . .
The sounds of people running free,
It will be time to eat,
And a place for you to meet,
The smell of food in the air,
I think I will sit on the chair,
The sound of the drinks machine,
And all the tables that are clean,
The noise of all the talking people,
and the lovely smell of treacle.
Now I had better go
before all the people start to show!

I am out here feeling the air,
It doesn't matter what I wear,
It will always be cold out here.
The wind is strong, it caused a tear.
All the seagulls flying round,
They give such a terrible sound.
Why does the weather have to be so bad?
It does make me feel so sad.
The sting of the wind which gives such pain,
And the terrible falling of the rain,
The weather makes me feel like cursing,
I can hear a van reversing,
Now I had better go,
In case it just might snow!

Alison Griffiths (13)
Lynn Grove GM High School

AUTUMN

An aroma of lovely things
Coming from the dining room.
When the lunch bell rings
The doors are flung open *Boom!*
It was nice and quiet
Before the kids came in
All things that they ate
And throwing food in the bin.
No one can go outside
Because it's pouring down with rain
They'll have to wait and wait
Until the sun comes out again.
It's really, really crowded
Because there's nowhere else to go
You've lost your friends, you can't escape
Because of a crowd that's going slow.
You've finally found your mates
They're sitting in the hall
There's nothing else to do
Apart from playing with a ball.
The wind went round the school
And it was really cold
Someone went out in the rain
Which we thought was really bold.
The bell rang so it was the end of lunch.
We were the last people out
And we said we'd meet after school
'Don't be late' I shout.
We did meet after school with a brolly I had to borrow.
It wasn't sunny today, well there's always tomorrow.

Katie White (12)
Lynn Grove GM High School

BEGINNING OF AUTUMN

As I walk outside the cold hits me,
I look around and I can see,
Lots of birds flying high.
Making their journeys through the sky.
Their wings are spread out, they're flying free,
High above me and over the trees.
Droplets of rain start to fall,
And in the distance I hear a bird call.
Squawking birds gliding from the rain to the shelter of trees
Then the wind gets colder and my fingers start to freeze.
The leaves from the trees are gliding through the air,
And the wind starts blowing through my hair,
I can see for miles over rooftops and trees.
And white, fluffy clouds floating above me.
Shining crystals are strung on the silky threads,
Of a tiny spider's glistening web.
The rain is still pattering to the ground,
And the trees are swaying without a sound.
As I stand there my toes are numb and cold,
I watch a bird searching for worms in the mould.
I hear lots of other birds making a din,
And the wind is flattening my clothes to my skin.
In the distance I can see smoky air,
Because of the smoke coming from chimneys there,
The wind is still whistling, the rain is still falling,
The trees are still swaying, and birds are still calling,
There is dew on the grass which glistens in the sun,
The weather tells me autumn has begun.

Sarah Ling (12)
Lynn Grove GM High School

AUTUMN

Step outside, eyes squinting in the wind
that blows at such a force.
Hair over your face, so you have difficulty
to see where you are going.
The ground, covered in dirty, murky puddles.
That children love to jump in so the water
splashes over them

The sky scattered with dark, grey, clouds,
it's going to rain.
You start to head home, the rain stings
as it hits your face.
The trees sway this way and that
with a sudden very ferocious gust of wind.
Leaves scatter everywhere like colours flying.

The rain soon stops, you stay out, you step on
some leaves that did not get wet,
they rustle and crunch under your feet.
You start to shiver as the wind gets
harder, you can't feel your fingers or toes,
you walk for a while.

look up, you see all the smoke coming from
chimneys of houses along the street, you are
suddenly filled with warmth as you pick up
speed to get home.

Charlene Burn (12)
Lynn Grove GM High School

IS IT A CURSE?

I watch from my window as the clouds pass by,
I see the seagulls flapping their wings and screeching
in search for food but there is none!
There are children outside playing, all wrapped up in coats,
but still they shiver as they feel the coldness rush against them.
Their hair blows strongly in front of their faces,
and their hands are so cold they are numb!
The drizzles of rain crash hard against my window,
it sends a shiver down my spine.
I look up and see the sky, it is grey and dull,
it reminds me of snow and the frosty icicles.
But it is not winter, so why bring bad weather?
It feels like a curse, so I ask myself why?
The trees blow wildly as the strong, strong wind passes though them,
and the branches are almost bare as the leaves have fallen off.
They look so cold and the wet rain dribbles off each individual leaf,
it looks as though they are crying!
And the trees themselves now look like bony old men,
all crooked and misshapen.
It's just a change from the beautiful flowers
that blossomed in the spring!
The sun shone like there was no end,
the land was dry, and there was brightly coloured, fresh green grass.
But now the puddles wait to be evaporated,
they wait and wait but still there is no sun,
when will this curse end?
Ask you now, not just for me,
when will we see the light of day again?

Sarah Kibble (12)
Lynn Grove GM High School

PRINGLES

P stands for Pringles,
R eally round and bare,
I n all different flavours,
N othing can compare.
G ood to taste,
L ovely to smell,
E asy to crunch,
S o pop a Pringle for your lunch.

Fallon Brownlie (12)
Lynn Grove GM High School

HATE IS . . .

Hate is red like fire burning away at logs,
It tastes like bitter coffee,
It smells like rotten vegetables,
Hate looks like the thorns on roses,
It sounds like breaking glass,
Hate feels cold and lonely.

Lee-Ann Philpott (13)
Lynn Grove GM High School

LOVE IS . . .

Love is the colour of the sea-blue sky,
Love is the sound of birds singing,
Love feels warm and cosy,
Love tastes like strawberries and cream,
Love smells like 'Lynx Africa',
Love looks like a single red rose on a thorn bush.

Trina Patel (13)
Lynn Grove GM High School

FEAR

Fear is pure black, the blacker the better,
Fear tastes like bile, bitter and vulgar,
Fear smells like burnt wood alone in a cold, dark forest,
Fear looks like a spooky road, dark and abandoned
                        with not a word to be heard,
Fear is a deathly silence, when you cannot move,
                        just tremble with fright,
Fear is something you can never get rid of,
. . . *It's in you forever!*

Danielle Kibble (13)
Lynn Grove GM High School

SUPER GRAN

When I am old I will eat junk food,
I will go to different pubs and drink different drinks except tea,
I will go on holidays no one would go on except me,
I will go clubbing every night,
I will have my ears pierced top to bottom,
I will listen to music, rock, pop, jazz and rave,
I will have straight hair,
I will not smell and won't have wrinkles,
I will dance until dawn and have parties on every occasion.
That's why I'm going to be a Super Gran!

Carolyn Stone (13)
Lynn Grove GM High School

What Is Love?

Love is the colour red, where we think of deep red hearts
                                    and red kissable lips.
Love tastes like fresh strawberries and cream.
Love smells like freshly opened fragrances.
Love looks like a couple snuggled close in the moonlight.
Love sounds like words said from the heart.
Love feels like a Pandora's box of emotions.

Victoria Barfield (13)
Lynn Grove GM High School

Football

F ans are shouting
O ut for their teams
O ff and on
T he players go
B ooked in anger
A ngry managers
L oudly shouting
L ots of noise.

Mitchell Faraday-Drake (12)
Lynn Grove GM High School

Rugby

R eally rough and the
U ltimate sport
G ot to be strong to play
B ecause you will get flattened
Y ou get muddy.

Jody Bailey (12)
Lynn Grove GM High School

OLD AND FUNKY!

When I'm old I am going to stand out
I'll go on holiday to a hot place
I will go out for meals and stuff my face
I'll wear weird clothes to everyone else
I'll go swimming in the sea and take a dingy
My house will be nice like gold and maroon and a colour of ice
I'll waste my money on silly things
I'll still have a love life
I won't have grey hair, I'll dye it red
And every day I'll lie on my waterbed.

Leah Bulloch (13)
Lynn Grove GM High School

CHOCOLATE

C aramel on top
H oney as well
O verlapping
C hocolate
O n the top
L ots
A nd lots of
T offee and
E at it all up.

Ryan Scott (12)
Lynn Grove GM High School

AUTUMN

A utumn is cold,
U nder trees leaves lay,
T rees go bare,
U ndressed they look,
M any leaves brown and orange,
N umb with cold you will get.

Daniel Harris (12)
Lynn Grove GM High School

FEAR!

Fear is grey, like a stone-cold path.
The taste is bitter like an old musty wine.
The smell is like a lonely, damp forest.
It looks like an old, empty theatre, (no actors in sight).
There is no sound, just silence.
The feel of fear is rough and cold.

Katherine Emmerson (13)
Lynn Grove GM High School

ANGER

Anger is crimson-red.
Anger tastes like an extremely hot curry.
Anger smells like rotten eggs.
Anger looks like hell.
Anger sounds like a train whistle.
Anger feels like a prickly thorn bush.

Stephen Allen (13)
Lynn Grove GM High School

HATE IS

Hate is black.
It tastes like overcooked liver and onions.
It smells like one thousand rotten eggs!
It looks like black, thick, slimy tar coughed
                    from a heavy smoker's lungs!
It sounds like an army marching with wet shoes!
It feels like cold, lumpy custard trickling down your body!

Ben Ablitt (13)
Lynn Grove GM High School

ANGER!

Anger is deep, dark red.
It tastes like raw onion that has been rolled in mud.
It smells like running sweat trickling down somebody's body.
It looks like blood oozing from a killed animal.
The sound is like everybody pounding your ears.
It's like being put in an electric chair!

John Beales (13)
Lynn Grove GM High School

POISON

Black is the colour of it.
It tastes lethal.
It smells deadly.
It looks oozy and runny.
It sounds bubbly.
It feels like hands choking you around your neck.

Shaun Lehan (13)
Lynn Grove GM High School

HAPPINESS IS . . .

Happiness is colour acid yellow,
Happiness smells like the perfume 'Forever',
Happiness looks like a huge great theme park,
Happiness sounds like the very sweet voices of children playing,
Happiness feels like flying in the air,
Happiness tastes like ripe juicy oranges.

Laura Philpot (13)
Lynn Grove GM High School

EMOTIONS

Emotions, emotions,
All kinds of emotions,
Red, hot, evil, anger,
Dark, black, vicious, hate,
Grey, musty fear,
Yellow, bright, flowery joy,
And last but not least pink, fiery, jealous love.

Carly Chatten (13)
Lynn Grove GM High School

OLD PEOPLE

When I am old I will buy a GTI sports car,
I will have a mansion in Ibiza,
I will drink whisky and lager,
I will go to America,
I will rob a bank,
And when I am old I will die.

Jason Gilham (13)
Lynn Grove GM High School

WHEN I GET OLD

When I get old I will get my hair permed.
I will wear high shoes.
I will wear fashionable clothes.
I will eat pizza for tea.
I will drink coffee.
I will eat chocolate.
I will go out for meals.
I will not drink tea.
I will eat pizza for breakfast.
I will knit toys for my grandchildren.

Samantha Norman (13)
Lynn Grove GM High School

A FIREWORK AS A THUNDERSTORM

Banging, crackling
Watch the bright colours flash by
Without a care in the world
Quickly they come and go
Watch it explode by candlelight
And feel the warmth of the glow

In the sky look out for the snapping and jumping
And you might be lucky enough to see the spectacular sight
The loud, bright, colourful flashes of the night.

Donna Turnbull (15)
Methwold High School

A Bond That Wasn't Strong Enough

Whilst in each other's company our actions caused pandemonium.
Perhaps it is a comfort for some,
That my shadow now walks,
Where my memory still sees you standing.

Instead of listening to your philosophical phrases,
Now I constantly hear the agonising echoes of our argument.
Our ultimate argument,
The one that stole our companionship from our possession.

Yesterday you were stood laughing in my shadow.
Today you sit thoughtfully,
In the silhouette of a grand, patriarchal oak tree.
The oak tree in which our initials remain,
Since the day we carved them deep into the bark.
Though the carving still exists,
Our once cherished friendship has been obliterated.

A deadly silence momentarily occupies the space where you stood.
Now I wonder if you weren't my guardian angel,
Teaching me that excruciating lesson,
'You never know what you've got until it's gone.'

Donna Greenacre (14)
Methwold High School

GROOVY GRAN!

My dear old gran is ninety one,
She thinks she's twenty two,
She bungee jumps and parachutes,
And paints her nails blue!

My dear old gran's a diamond,
She really is a gem,
She's rescued seven stray cats,
And kept each one of them.

Last year's London Marathon,
My gran, she thought she'd run,
No one thought she'd make it,
That was until she won!

Some people think Gran's fashion sense,
Is strange to say the least,
Some of the trends she uses,
Have long since been deceased.

She's got these awful leggings,
The shade of mouldy cheese,
She wears them with her platform boots,
That come up to her knees.

Her living room is painted,
With gold and silver stars,
She has a papier mâché sun,
Mercury and Mars.

Her motorbike's her pride and joy,
She rides it everywhere,
She wears a bright green helmet,
On top of purple hair.

I know that she's eccentric,
Perhaps behind the times,
But I still love my grandma,
She's fully in her prime!

Rachel Marsland (15)
Methwold High School

NIGHTMARE

As the sun retires from the dying day,
Darkness spreads his ghoulish hand,
Terror and Despair come out to play
And devour the orange lit land.

Darkness creeps up, fuels my fears,
Lurking, lingering, slyly in wait,
Sinister breathing smites my ears,
Taunting me before he seals my fate.

Digging, digging, always digging,
Deeper, deeper, but in vain,
I glance back up, see why I'm digging,
For the tombstone spells out my name.

I feel the pain of a thousand knives
As I fall, pleading at his feet,
The reaper swings his blood-stained scythe,
And awakens me from my hellish sleep.

Joe Newell (16)
Methwold High School

SLAVERY

I am in pain
As the whip hits
The knuckles of my hand
See the blood running down my ripped trousers.
And my legs are freezing
As cold as my face.
I was very, very frightened because
I kept getting hit with a whip.
And I didn't get much food.
I only got two drinks and one slice of bread.
And my tummy was rumbling
And because I was not getting much food.
I want to run away
From my evil master
So soon I will try and escape
And see my family, and be healthy.

James Stubbins (12)
Methwold High School

THE HURT POLAR BEAR

What happened to the polar bear was really not fair,
The irresponsible old hunter had left out a snare.
The polar bear would have lost its paw,
Except that a police man came, friend of the law.
He finally tracked down the clumsy old man,
And he was sent off in a police van.
Soon his trial came and he was sent to 'the clink',
All this just because he did not think.

Ed Hendry (13)
Reepham High School

A POEM

Leaping salmon,
Whispering leaves,
Laughing water,
Murm'ring breeze.
Growing grass,
Singing lark,
Golden corn,
Listening dark.
Silver moon,
Gentle rain,
Shining sun,
Standing grain.
Deep, still mill-pond,
Mouthing carps,
Falling water
Sounds like harps.
Hovering Merlin,
Nervous mice,
Snow in winter,
Slippery ice.
Cold, grey dawn-light,
Diamond dew,
Whistling starling,
Morning new.

Lauren Orton (13)
Reepham High School

TIME TRAVEL

A mysterious event with cause unknown,
You stand in twisted time alone.

Many years are left behind,
But more ahead there are to find.

Decades pass by through darkness and light,
Day disappears into gathering night.

Through time and space pass the ages,
Enough to fill a book with pages.

Time is eternal, it is vast,
You travel from present to future and past.

You travel through time with sight and speed,
Taking no heed of history's deeds.

Many lives pass before your eyes,
Time is full of riddles and lies.

Time is a sea full of ages,
You travel on it as its water rages.

Through lands unknown you pass alone,
Through years and ages where fears have grown.

Stages are ready for time to unfold,
To tell its stories of new and old.

Time is a story you travel through it,
It has no start, it has no end for the bell is ringing
That present is past and future beginning.

Sarah Boycott (13)
Reepham High School

THAT BIKE

That old bike been there for years,
And no one cares,
When I drive past,
I don't drive fast,
I think of that old bike,
It's a red old thing,
And it looks like it's got wings,
So I thought of taking it home,
So I did,
And you know, it made it look like new,
Then one day I came home,
The old thing had gone,
'Oh well,' I said,
'I will miss that old bike.'

Jenna Brett (13)
Reepham High School

FOOTBALL MANIA

F ootball fun for everyone,
O h yes even a nun,
O nly professionals play on TV,
T ons of people play in the fantasy.
B alls, loads of footballs flying into the net,
A lways support your local team,
L ots of footy fans that's supreme,
L oads and loads of football mania that's the theme.

Ben Sharrod (13)
Reepham High School

TEENAGE LIFE

My brother is annoying
life is boring
being a teenager can get you down.

When I go out with my friends
my mother goes round the bend
cos I have not done my chores
my God look at what it can cause.

When my father gets in he argues
with my mother,
they never stop, it gets me down.

Sometimes I just sit in a corner
trying to ignore them, it doesn't work.
Sometimes I even cry myself to sleep
cos it gets me down that much.
I can't wait till I leave home.

Sam Marshall (13)
Reepham High School

NATURAL

The natural world is full of splendour
The birds and bees of all different gender
But in this world the most beautiful thing
Is you in a bikini and a red rubber ring.

Charles Flack (14)
Reepham High School

ME!

C razy child.
A bsolutely talkative.
R avishing person.
R ight rebel.
I ncredible.
E ntertainer to all humans.

J iffy jester.
A lways goes red.
C aring kid.
K nobbly knees.
S weet as candy.
O riginal minx.
N ow look at her 'What do you think?'

Carrie Jackson (13)
Reepham High School

DYING

Blood everywhere as far as the eye can see.
Bodies as far as the horizon.
Craters scattered on the floor like autumn leaves.
Shells going off like Christmas crackers one by one.
My friend lay dead next to me.
Still as a tree on a hot summer's night.
Wounded walking on the path of the forgotten.
Having conversations with those who no longer exist.
A sharp stab in the back I felt.
Then I knew,
I knew what was going to happen,
I was going to join those who do not exist anymore.

Benjamin Harrison (13)
Rosemary Musker High School

DEADLY OBSESSION

He saw the new girl, sitting alone,
He was sitting in his own shadow, staring at her shimmering beauty.

He walked home alone that night, humiliated,
He had loved her, and she had laughed!
She wasn't as angelic as she had first seemed,
But he knew how to convert her.

The next day, he followed her after school;
The cold, autumn darkness closed in.
He followed her all the way to her ordinary home,
He did not leave that night, he skulked in her garden,
The darkness thickened, the moon pushed its way through angry clouds.

She sat up suddenly in her bed, sweating,
He was standing in her room, cloaked in an aura of evil,
It choked her and made her feel nauseous.
He glided forward slowly, purposefully,
The stench of pure evil suffocated her,
She wished that this would just be a bad dream,
She covered her nose and mouth to stop herself from screaming.

He smiled, and she saw his fangs glinting in the moonlight,
His yellow, clawed hand reached forward.
As quick as an animal, she grabbed the old, wooden stake,
Without warning, she thrust it deep into his chest,
His eyes opened wide and his mouth dropped open with surprise,
The vampire died silently, crumbling to dust.

The evil flew about the room, confused,
She opened the window, and the evil evaporated.
The bright sun rose, lighting up the world,
Surprised, she held up her hands in a futile defence,
She screamed, her fangs a brilliant white,
The vampire crumbled to dust.

Lee Anderson (13)
Rosemary Musker High School

HIDING

As the shroud of twilight comes over,
The heart screams of black desires.
My home towers over their village like a hand reaching out.
The town is covered with mist like a cobweb.
The people are like rabbits, hiding in burrows,
Trying to shelter from the claws of fear.
Their hiding doesn't fool me, I have eyes like the hawk,
And the same killer instinct.
Like the vulture I prey on the weak,
And like the gods I am immortal.
Sunlight being the only thorn in my side.
As I leave the town my dark reign dissolves,
Leaving only a remnant of terror
That had engulfed the hiding town.

Adam Giverin (13)
Rosemary Musker High School

THE SUN

The sun stones us with treacherous heat.
It burns like a burning flame.
The sun is our idol,
Although we don't care.
Everyone moans about it,
They say it's too hot, too sunny,
Just think if there was no sun,
You wouldn't get a lovely day,
You wouldn't have light.
You would have to have street lights everywhere.
You wouldn't see a thing.
So remember when you say it's too hot, too sunny.
The sun protects us from the day and it also keeps us warm.

Michelle Bailey (13)
Rosemary Musker High School

SILENT ARMY

The clear night sky with the stars ever watching overhead,
The moonlight casting shadows, very silent.
Watching the old building like a hunter watches its prey,
Creeping up very slowly, oh so slowly.

The door slams open like thunder in a storm,
Quick! Duck! Before our cover's blown.
There is the signal to move, quick, come on,
Like snakes slithering in the grass.

Sweating buckets, eyes stinging, heart pounding like a drum.
Quick, we're spotted! Get out of here! Back to camp!
Racing along as if a tiger was pursuing me,
It seems as though I've been running for hours.

Camp!
Feels like heaven!
Mission failed though,
God, help!

Philip Clayton (13)
Rosemary Musker High School

DREAM MAN

He appears only in my dreams,
He's tall, gentle and fine,
Perfect or so it seems,
Easy to notice his radiant shine.
He's been sent from above,
He fills my heart with glee.
He's my undying love,
For he forever burns in me.

There's no end and no start,
He floats in and out like a feather.
He'll always hold a place in my heart,
I only wish we could be together.
With one look into his big blue eyes,
I could lose myself forever and always.
Without words he answers my tender cries,
Before returning to my soul where he stays.

Lynsey McKay (13)
Rosemary Musker High School

HIDING

The paws of the wolf patting on the ground
sounding like heavy rain is getting nearer breath by breath.
I can already hear it growling and now the cold bites my toes,
I know I've got to hide.
Up a tree with bony arms or in a haunted house, that's the one.
As I race up to the door with the wolf on my tail
I hope I can hide before I'm blood and bones.
As the door opens it groans and creaks like an ancient coffin
but at last I'm in as I slam the door shut!
Now I'm running through a maze of spider webs
trying to hide before the wolf comes hurrying in.
I'll hide in the cupboard with the big black bats
watching me with eyes like headlights.
It growls and grunts as it walks past the stairs
and into the silent night like a demon from hell.
So I pick up my courage and run out of the house,
afraid of the creatures waiting outside.

Emma Rutherford (13)
Rosemary Musker High School

MY UNKNOWN LOVER

I look at him,
But nobody knows,
I secretly love him,
But on life goes.

I see him at school,
If I catch his eyes,
He usually stops,
And sometimes says 'Hi.'

We chat for a while,
Then he will go.
How I feel,
He doesn't know.

One thing I know,
And this is true,
One day I'll stop him,
And say 'I love you.'

But for now,
I won't tell another.
And for the moment he'll stay,
My unknown lover.

Sarah Read (14)
Rosemary Musker High School

HEARTBREAK

Your heart is broken
Smell violent, scarlet roses
Sitting in front of the fire
Craving for your lover.

Daniel Eke (13)
Rosemary Musker High School

TO RISE IS TO FALL

Radiant sunset in the sky,
To the daytime say goodbye.
Look to the sky and the clouds above,
To a world of peace, harmony, lust and love.

Hark can you hear the peaceful sound?
Harmonic music all around.
Meeting people pure and white,
Who then decide if it's day or night.

Day is gracious soft and warm,
Night is cold and full of gloom.
Will you rise or will you fall?
To a dark damp cave and a gaping wall?

Pleading with the tenants, I am good, I swear,
Please say my judgement will be fair.
Whatever is decided I'll be alright,
I hope the murky darkness becomes white light.

For here I am and forever on,
With an elegant white horse to ride upon.
Praise the lord for being fair,
To let me up into his air.

Thank the devil with a frown,
For he will not weigh me down.

Hannah Long (14)
Rosemary Musker High School

WAR

In 1914 the Great War started,
Families were split up and lovers parted.
Posters were put up to get men to fight,
To throw themselves into that terrible plight.
The soldiers came from far and wide,
Their families' hearts filled with fear and pride.
Many of them went to lend a hand,
Wandering dangerously across No Man's land.
So many of them were dying and hurt,
Laid to rest upon the dirt.
The trenches were muddy holes in the ground,
Where soldiers could sleep and hope not to be found.
So few lived to the end of the war,
Some knew not what they were fighting for.
Some were not men at all but boys,
Who thought of weapons of war as toys.
Soldiers were captured, tortured and killed,
Every day innocent blood was spilled.
Women got messages that their loved ones were gone,
The slaughter of lives went on and on.
Then to one side victory came,
The world would never be the same.
So when the war did finally end,
The people had the world to mend.
When at last peace was resolved,
They remembered the brave and the bold.

Amanda Douglass (14)
Rosemary Musker High School

HIDING

Can they see me?
I'd better hide
Charging like a pack of bulls
Guns banging like fireworks
The sun is boiling
I lie down, flat as an envelope
Running like the wind they try to find me.

Their green tanks and suits look very camouflaged
Like trees in the forest.
I'm the bull's eye, they're aiming at me
Like a dart board but no it's me!

Feet banging on the grass
Like a fleet of sheep playing the brass
I lie still, as still as a mouse
No one can find me behind this little house.

Kate Wood (13)
Rosemary Musker High School

MAKE ME A WEREWOLF!

Make me a werewolf strong and bold.
The terror a like of young and old.
Grant me a figure tall and spare
The speed of a leopard, the claws of a bear.
The poison of snakes, the wit of a fox.
The stealth of the wolf, the strength of the ox.
The jaws of a tiger, the teeth of a shark.
The eyes of a cat that sees in the dark.

Lucy Palfrey (13)
Rosemary Musker High School

KEEP ON GOING

Slowly, quietly, you creep along,
Step after step like the beat of song.
Maybe you'll live, maybe you'll die,
But whatever it takes you'll have to stay sly.
You're startled by a noise just ahead,
And cower with fear in case it's the Head.
But you don't need to worry, it's just a group of boys,
They're just trying to find Mrs Dikoy.
At last they have gone and you're back on track,
Under the tables and past the coat rack.
At last you think you made it,
But you still have far to go.
Keep on creeping and hiding,
Till at last you're finally home.

Kerry-Ann Wells (13)
Rosemary Musker High School

SNOWFLAKES

S now is falling all around,
N ow I'm slipping to the ground.
O ver hills and on my feet,
W hat happened to the summer heat?
F olk are rushing to get home,
L ikely they'll eat more than bone.
A ll around the world is ice,
K nife-edged cold is not too nice.
E verything is white and plain,
S oon it will be warm again.

Joanne Shepherd (13)
Rosemary Musker High School

MY TREE

One spring I planted an acorn,
I dug it a small hole,
And that became its home,
By the time summer came,
My acorn had a shoot,
The shoot was only 6cm tall.
But mum said it would die in the winter,
My mum was wrong.
When autumn came I dug it up,
And moved it to a plant pot,
Then took it to my room.
I watered it every day,
But only one drop.
November came it was 12cm tall.
At Christmas I showed it my presents.
Spring came it was 15cm tall.
Mum told me to put it outside again,
And that's what I did.
This winter I did not take it in, it was too big.
Now I am 13 and my acorn tree,
Is still standing there taller than me!

Samantha Rowntree (13)
Rosemary Musker High School

RED

Dying roses
Body lying in the field
Blood trickling down his face
Fire burning around him
The sun setting for last time for the man.

Marcus Leeder (13)
Rosemary Musker High School

SEA

Sun-swept sand and seagulls squawking,
Skies gleaming,
Sailboat streaming,
In the smooth sea.

Sun sinking, stars rising,
Sea swallowing,
Starfish from the soggy sand,
Sails flapping into the red sky.

Sticky sweaty skin on the sunny beach,
The sea reflecting the sun,
Never staying still.

Stuart Coulson (13)
Rosemary Musker High School

RED

Red is a raging fire,
Glowing in the night.
Red is growing anger,
Exploding into a fight.
Red is for love,
Passionate and flirting.
Red is for blood,
Spilling out and spurting.
Red is for a rose,
A symbol of affection.
And red is a cross,
For world-wide protection.

Ashley Byford (13)
Rosemary Musker High School

SNAKE

His tongue like a worm ripping into you.
The eyes he has are red as dripping blood.
His body is longer than a twenty foot ruler.
The body is long, thick as shining bright gold.
His tail will strike when you pray for a striker to strike his tail.
His teeth are sharper than a shark and shining bones.
The colours on him are like a rainbow with more colours.

Adam Moon (14)
Rosemary Musker High School

EAGLE

Eyes like piercing lazer
As fast as lightning
Feathers as soft as down
As swift as the wind
Claws as sharp as razors.

James Miller (14)
Rosemary Musker High School

AT WAR

Pouring with blood as the devil laughed.
My heart was pounding with anger.
Danger was in front of me.
There I stood. Looking down
At my Grandad's grave.

Carl Bedford (13)
Rosemary Musker High School

SUMMER

Sitting in the sun,
Watching the clouds go by,
The sun is shining down my back,
People laughing,
Children playing,
The smell of barbecues,
All around,
Going out on trips,
Having picnics.

Going on holidays,
In the summer sun,
Beaches and sandcastles,
The sea and ice-cream,
Time to go home,
On this hot and bothered day.

Susan McCambridge (14)
Rosemary Musker High School

EAGLE

Eyes as round as marbles
Feathers as soft as fur
As swift as an arrow
Flies as high as a plane
Beak as sharp as scissors.

Kim Barker (13)
Rosemary Musker High School

PEACEFULNESS

Close your eyes gently
And cuddle in,
Keep yourself snug
A new day will begin.

Have pleasant dreams
About those things you love,
Sleep is an island
Waiting above.

Night is a blanket
Keeping you warm,
If you close your eyes
You can come to no harm.

Dreams are like journeys
Drifting along,
Rest is a present
Keeping you strong.

Laura Taylor (13)
Rosemary Musker High School

SHATTERED LOVE

Bloody as a dead man
Whose love has lost
His heart is broken like shattered glass
His anger was as hot as burning wood.

Jonathan Wingrove (13)
Rosemary Musker High School

GEMMA

They're going off on holiday
That's plain for all to see
They're going off on holiday
And they're not taking me.

There are cases in the hallway
And beach toys for the sea
They've got a week, no work just play
But they're not taking me.

They're loading up the car
With sandwiches and tea
They'll be travelling very far
But they're not taking me.

Where are they going to put me?
How lonely will I be?
The house all looks so empty
Why aren't they taking me?

But look, here's more
My bed and bowls and meat
What are they doing? I'm not sure
Perhaps they're taking me.

My things are going in the car
My tail wags, for all to see
I don't care if they do go far
Because they're taking me.

Kelly Horgan (13)
Rosemary Musker High School

THE BATTLE

Wizards and dragons and treasures galore,
Stones of magic washed ashore.
Pools of gold, silver and bronze,
And these are the fruit of elfish songs.

Orcs, goblins, trolls and dark lords,
With their multitudes of evil hordes.
Hobbits with daggers and men with swords,
Some which are spies and some which are frauds.

Bracelets of magic, rings and lockets,
Things which greedy men like to put in their pockets.
Men in their armour, swords by their side,
Attack at dawn in boats on the tide.

Salted meat, stale bread,
These are the things that soldiers are fed.
Oily water, barrels of ale,
Of course the next day they turn out pale.

Evil magic, red magic, magic galore,
Perhaps not all from the times of yore,
Cars, pollution, bombs and guns,
Killing all of the father's sons.

The battle is won, the battle is lost,
But then again at what great cost,
Men go home to meet their wives,
Or remain in battle without their lives.

Danny Dyball (11)
St Nicholas Middle School, Great Yarmouth

WHAT IS IT ABOUT COCKNEYS?

Whether it's your 'apples and pairs'
Or your 'Barnet fairs'.
Just tell me . . .
What is it about cockneys?

Why is it 'a frog and toad'
And not just a road?
For God's sake . . .
What is it about cockneys?

Why do they take 'a butcher's hook'
When it's simpler to take a look.
Please . . .
What is it about cockneys?

Since when has a 'jam jar'
Ever been a car.
Somebody help me . . .
What is it about cockneys?

But just think if I didn't know 'em
I wouldn't have done this poem.
I wish someone would tell me . . .
What is it about cockneys?

Steven Creasey (16)
Thorpe St Andrew High School

TOWN WITHOUT SOUL

Town without soul.
Age without heart.
Beat me and starve me,
And tear me apart.
The grey walls of fear
Close in left and right,
And a million cruel eyes
Will mock me tonight.
The pale, faceless people
Of vodka and smoke
March on screaming 'Progress!'
To smother and choke.
The search for identity,
Something that's real,
Makes a prisoner of truth
And a hash of ideals.
The dregs of the future
Sign up on the dole.
Age without heart.
Town without soul.

Rebecca Gotts (17)
Thorpe St Andrew High School

LITTLE PERSONIFICATION

This poem is short
This poem is sweet
Compared to a person
It would be their feet.

Mark Thompson (17)
Thorpe St Andrew High School

WILD WIND

A wild wind blows,
it echoes through the dark oaks,
casting eerie shadows,
making dangerous shapes
across the forest floor.

The leaves rush in circles,
scattering and dancing,
drifting and floating
all around the giant oak,
which ruled the forest.

An old rotten tree made its last moves,
before crashing to the ground,
scattering birds and squirrels,
acorns and leaves.

The wind dies.
Silence.

Jennie Reeve (16)
Thorpe St Andrew High School

HIGHLAND MAGIC

Beauty and peace on the magical hills,
The water shimmers, so tranquil and still.
The sun gently fades behind the mountain range,
The air feels cool, the day's about to change.
Mountain springs glisten and so refreshing,
Views of the loch are spiritually breathtaking.

There's a coolness and fresh aroma in the air,
Disturbance here is extremely rare.
This place gives you that time needed to reflect,
There's no other place that could be so perfect.

Rebecca Hall (17)
Thorpe St Andrew High School

FLYING BUTT MONKEYS

That will
teach the
fool.
How *dare* he
turn down *my*
request.
For *five hundred*
billion dollars,
of government funding.
Doesn't he realise
how *important*
it is?
Adding more butts
to monkeys
is the future
of mankind.

Miaow, miaow
chicken
yellow
red, black.

Tim Cheesman (16)
Thorpe St Andrew High School

DESPERATE

How come almost everyone comes alone?
But when it echoes no one feels pain in the stomach?
A fat belly can be felt, but runny noses and tears dribble down.
Although it feels big, the pain comes back;
Straining to see with the squeaky car break eyes!
Tears again, uncomfort and dribbles;
I wish I could stay here and now forever.
Car door slams, no movement, dog feet, gates, keys, cracks!
Then . . . flush, all gone, no remains.
Coming down stairs, I wish I could be here forever.
Lights on and off, voices, mascara!
Silver, chopping, where?
What's going on? Please tell me; I'm all alone,
All terribly, terribly alone.

Georgina Durrant (17)
Thorpe St Andrew High School

COMPUTER TECHNOLOGY

Switch on the computer,
Logging on in style,
With a super-powered modem,
Already to dial.

Tapping on the keyboard,
Surfing the net,
With the world-wide web,
And a cute cyber pet.

The world is in your hands,
By the click of the mouse,
You can chat to many people,
In the comfort of your house.

Communicating by E-mail,
The amazing CD ROM,
Technology at its best,
www.end@uk.com.

Jenny Pearce (17)
Thorpe St Andrew High School

FINDING INSPIRATION

I tried to write a poem while lying in bed
But the words just would not flow into my head.
I tried to write it when watching TV
But that was totally wrong for me.
I sat in a field and tried to think
But couldn't write because of the stink.
I sat on a log in a lonely glade,
The sun was bright so I moved to the shade.
Under a tree I began to write
But a bird flew by and gave me a fright.
I ran to a park and sat on a swing
But by then I couldn't think of a thing.
So I went back home and had some toast
And began to write about what I know most.
What I've been through to complete this rhyme
And bring it to you, finished in time.

Sarah Hill (18)
Thorpe St Andrew High School

LOSING YOU

We walked side by side
And laughed together,
Laughed for ages over things no one else would find funny.
You kept tickling me (even though you knew I hated it)
And telling me your little jokes.
Despite the fact I'd heard them all before
You still made me laugh. You always can
We talked for hours as always -
On the phone it was just the same.
That day we just sat, chatting away.
We can talk about anything, you and me.
That's one of the things I love about you.
We know each other so well
But it's hard when we're apart.
It twists me up inside
When I think about you far away.
But not that day. We were so happy
Just the two of us together.
The time went by so fast,
Then I had to go, all too soon.
You kissed me softly when you said goodbye,
Everything was perfect.
Then I woke to find that happened long ago
And we were finished.
There was no 'you and me' anymore.
'Just good friends' you said.
It's hard to just be friends
After giving everything you could.
I can't help it, I still miss you.
I got up for school with a heavy heart.

Rosie Ledwidge (16)
Thorpe St Andrew High School

MURDERED BY MADNESS - HITLER'S VICTIMS

Ant-like in their numbers in their stride
Marching, conforming, stripped of their pride
Under the thumb of a severed hand
All dreaming the fantasy of a harmonious land.

Its mouth was opened and ready to grind
Unbolted from societies subconscious mind
Condemned tortured souls were now free in the wind
Revengeful in the knowledge of the hand that had sinned.

Conflict and control makes our world go round
And the powerless majorities can't make a sound.

Sara Eltringham (17)
Thorpe St Andrew High School

ASPECTS OF LIFE!

Everything blossoms from the bud of life
The angry husband, the screaming wife
The playful child in the street
The everyday people that you always meet
The homeless people in despair
The business types who do not care
The loving couple with each other
The crying baby with its mother
The desirable man in his prime
The immature pupils wasting time
The idealistic stars on TV
Then of course there's also me!

Paula Harwood (17)
Thorpe St Andrew High School

IS ALL LOST?

When something can not be found,
When something is lost,
When it falls away,
What does it cost?

It costs the happiness of a family,
It looses your father to a drink,
All the things that were once almost perfect,
All begin to fall and sink.

On soft, luscious lips,
A once sweet, tender kiss,
Is torn away,
It becomes something to miss.

Looking into innocent eyes,
And what can you see?
Children who are frightened,
How safe can they be?

An old man lies half dead on the road,
Sprawled and fallen into brown mud,
No one stops and helps him up,
They just stand and watch the dripping red blood.

A tear trickles down a pale little face,
Because now it's lost it can not be found,
As we begin to run the unbeatable race
Nothing can be heard, not a sound.

Jennifer Bateman (17)
Thorpe St Andrew High School

STEALING NINE

What a disgrace
Leave me alone, I want to live
You better run, run,
All doom and gloom,
Nothing will stun.

Death is your faith
Never finding happiness,
Take off in space
Too much negativity
Hiding behind your face.

Fascists by the book
I see something I can't break.
Pick me, pick me,
Waiting for the punchline
Waiting to be free.

Barry Maynard (16)
Thorpe St Andrew High School

TIGER

His whiskers as thin as cotton,
His teeth like blades,
Eyes like fire,
Fur as smooth as silk,
Ears listening for the deadly pounce,
Fierce and deadly is his pounce,
Roar as loud as screams,
Sending shock waves through you,
Claws like knives,
And before you know it, you're
Dead!

Neal Hartle (11)
Thorpe St Andrew High School

MY RABBIT

I have a rabbit
Thumper's his name,
My friend has one,
Exactly the same.

I love . . .
Their cute, fluffy, cotton tails,
Their lovely, black, long ears,
Their shiny, silky, soft fur,
And the way they have no fears.

They both love food,
Carrots and the ripe grape,
They have black and white spots,
Even the same shape!

I love the way they bounce,
And their cute, button noses,
When you give them a bath,
They smell like sweet roses.

Lovely little rabbits,
I love all your habits!

Rachel Harvey (11)
Thorpe St Andrew High School

22 MEN, 1 ROUND OBJECT AND 2 GOAL POSTS

As I stand, drowning in a sea of supporters,
I witness a mixture of tribal aggressions,
Many deep desires flowing from within countless hearts,
Endless bellowing, screaming, chanting and singing,
 am surrounded by a stadium, watching their team.

As one side gain an advantage, their fans erupt
Into an unrivalled ecstasy, jeering and laughing
The opposition then fall quiet, devastated
Sometimes I wonder how so much emotion rides,
On 22 men, 1 round object and 2 goal posts.

Ben Kennedy (16)
Thorpe St Andrew High School

PIG

Its body is a bouncy ball
near to the ground.
It's not very tall,
its tail's the shape
of a bouncy spring,
only it feels like a bit of string.
Its nose is like a big round button,
it has tiny whiskers
like strands of cotton.
Its ears are torn old bits of cloth
and when it eats it really scoffs.
Its trotters are like
old wooden clothes pegs.
Compared to their body
they have skinny legs.
They live in a sty
their skin is pink
and very often they really stink!

Natalie Bush (12)
Thorpe St Andrew High School

MINI!

Its exhaust a machine gun,
Its engine a purring cat,
Its headlights two clean-cut crystals,
Its bumper a black balloon,
When waxed it's a hot chick.

Eddie Quick (12)
Thorpe St Andrew High School

A RABBIT

A rabbit's whiskers are threads of soft cotton.
Its fur a soft comfy cushion.
Their ears pointed thorns.
Its tail like a ball of wool,
Its nose some soft corn.

Adam Jones (11)
Thorpe St Andrew High School

THE LAND ROVER

Its engine like a roaring beast,
Its power underestimated,
It only moves at low speeds,
But with a steady crawl it conquers all.
With a BHP of one hundred and two,
It says a lot about itself to me and you.

Jonathan Robert Hunt (11)
Thorpe St Andrew High School

MY CAT

Its eyes as green as grass
Its fur as soft as silk
Its tongue a piece of sandpaper
Its purr a never-ending rattle
Its nose like a little pink button
Its eyes two perfect almonds
Its ears two pieces of velvet
Its tail a fluffy bush
Its whiskers pieces of wire
It eats like a hungry tiger
It plays with anything it can find
It runs faster than the wind
When it goes to bed it always sleeps on something soft.

Alice Jackson (11)
Thorpe St Andrew High School

THE KITTEN

His fur is like a ball of wool
His tail, a straight stiff whip
His whiskers short and pointy
His nose a pale pink
His eyes are like beaming lights
His mouth is short and thin
His paws are soft and gentle
His claws are sharp, like pins
His ears, pointy triangles
His tummy, soft and warm
His teeth are long, thin daggers
But he'd never do me harm.

Juliet Chambers (11)
Thorpe St Andrew High School

A TIGER

Its fur pattern an army suit.
Its tail a furry whip.
Its teeth as sharp as a saw.
Its legs as strong as bricks.
It hunts just like a hound dog.
Its as quiet as a mouse.
Its nose a furry button.
Its mouth as big as a house.
Its ears are like sound detectors.
It runs like a car.
Its eyes can see for miles.
It pounces from so far.

Josie Gripton (11)
Thorpe St Andrew High School

HIPPO

Scoop it up, dig it out,
I need a place to doze,
The mud and dirt is everywhere,
It's going up my nose.

To excavate is to create,
A squelchy place to wallow,
A place to be with muddy mates,
Down where the ground is hollow.

Benjamin Drew (12)
Thorpe St Andrew High School

A DOG

Its tail is like a slithery snake.
Its nose is full of water.
Its ears a brush, brushing on the floor.
Its fur a ball of wool on the ground.
Its paws as big as shoes.
Its body a lovely golden brown.
Its eyes a twinkle in the moonlight.
Its legs furry and thin.
Its teeth are a very sharp knife.
Chewing at the doors.
Its tongue long, wet and dripping.
I take the doggy for walks.
Its bark is a loud noise.

Kelly Burns (11)
Thorpe St Andrew High School

FOOTBALL

I'm mad about football, it's the game for me
I've kicked a ball since the age of three.
I play for the school and the local team
Coming home dirty which makes mum scream.
I watch it on telly and dream of it too
To become a professional would be too good to be true.
I'll keep on playing as long as I can
Even when I become a man.
A team called Liverpool is the one for me
But I'll finish now because it's time for tea.

Ben Walsh (11)
Thorpe St Andrew High School

THE SHARK

As fast as a jet
And as bold as a tank
Not to be used as a prank.

As big as a bus
And its fin like a sail
If you see one you may pale.

Its teeth are like spears
So open your ears
If one's near
You better have fear.

It's twelve feet long
Big and grey
Scary and ferocious
Killing everything in its way.

Noel Howes (12)
Thorpe St Andrew High School

A DOG

A dog playful and sweet,
A cuddly ball of fur that sits on your feet.
The best friend of his owner who always wins him over.
He runs to greet but never manages to stay on his feet.
The member of the family that does not groan and complain
Especially in the pouring rain.
The one that cheers you up when you are low.
A friend indeed when you're in need.

Daniel Wittred (11)
Thorpe St Andrew High School

THE DOG

The yellow labrador sprinted through the forest,
Leaping at every lump and dip,
Then started to slow down dramatically,
To pick up the dark brown stick.

When it was in his jaw,
He came running back,
He darted to the left,
To which his owner lost track.

The owner was unhappy,
And sat on a log,
He felt a lick on his face,
Looked round . . . and saw his dog.

James Robert Dunthorne (11)
Thorpe St Andrew High School

CATS

Their whiskers strands of thread,
Thei r tongues as rough as sandpaper.
Their food that smells like mouldy bread,
Their noses wet, pink buttons.
Their toys spread all over the floor,
Their eyes sparkly marbles.
Their bodies a ball of cotton wool,
Their ears tiny, pointy triangles.

Zoe Franklin (11)
Thorpe St Andrew High School

THE ROLLER-COASTER

I hear people screaming,
When I'm in the queue,
My heart's beating faster,
Whatever shall I do?

Everyone is waiting
My turn is very near,
I've got to be so brave,
To conquer my great fear.

My eyes are tightly shut now,
We are going very fast,
I'm feeling awfully sick,
How long does this last?

My legs are very shaky,
But will I ever learn?
I rush forward to the queue,
To have another turn.

Gemma Clare (11)
Thorpe St Andrew High School

AN ART SET!

The paints are the sunset,
The crayons are too,
The scissors, sharpeners, pencils and glue.
The pens are a rainbow,
Great colours they show,
Biros and writing pads,
Highlighters that glow!

Andrew Love (11)
Thorpe St Andrew High School

WE LOST

I tried my hardest, I really did.
It wasn't my fault, blame it on Sid.
He handled their crosses in an awful way
It really wasn't his day.

The striker was out for the kill.
It only ended sixteen-nil.
We need a good manager rather than him,
Putting Billy up front was rather dim.

Maybe I should take up another sport,
Or maybe that knitting set mum bought.
But thinking about it win or lose
Football will always be the sport I choose.

John Habershon (11)
Thorpe St Andrew High School

WHAT'S OUTSIDE THE CLASSROOM WINDOW?

Through the classroom window I can see,
Tall, thin trees looking like guards with huge feather hats.
The sunlight touching the top of the hill
With grass fringes protecting the stubby stick fence.

But not a stir in sight
No mouse nor bird can be seen.
Until . . . *brrring, brrring* the school bell rings
Suddenly the sparrows and blackbirds swoop down like witches on
Broomsticks to pick up food from the busy playground.

That's all I could see!

Rachel Peck (12)
Wymondham College

A SONNET

Walking through the old trees, winter is near.
Wind and rain and ice, with the snow I fear.

Treading through the wet grass with the dew on top.
With time running past me, no time to stop.

Crisply frozen leaves, crunching under feet.
Children leave their homes, to the frosty street.

Laughter, shouting, shrill of joy, on to school.
A shame for ducks to swim, on icy pool.

Thick woolly hats and scarves with gloves on hands.
Slip and slide around, difficult to stand.

Rosy cheeks and noses blue from cold air.
Into school hurry up, no time to stare.

Look the sun has come out, and the ice will melt.
No more sliding now oh, how sad we felt.

Charlotte McDouall (14)
Wymondham College

THE HUMMING BIRD

In the tropics of the Arizona
A tiny bird of metallic colours
Roams the forest high and low
For food to make him slowly grow.

Nectar oozes from the flower
Glistening in the sunlight's power
The tiny bird arrives at speed
It's humming wings beat out its needs.

Poised, its long tongue delves and flicks
Into the depths of trumpeted sticks
Fulfilled the bird turns to fly away
It's gone on the breeze of the Arizona day.

Matthew Woodhouse (13)
Wymondham College

RAIN

The rain is on my window,
The rain is on the street,
I hear the pitter-patter
Of the rain's steady beat.

It's splashing in the puddles,
It's splashing on the grass,
I have to stay inside today
No time to have a laugh

The rain is pounding hard now,
Never to stop again
I can hardly see outside now,
Out of the windowpane.

It's starting to calm down now,
The clouds are starting to clear,
The sun is starting to shine
The rain I can no longer hear now.

It's a nice day now,
The birds are flying free,
I could go outside now
But that's completely up to me.

Sarah-Louise Robinson (13)
Wymondham College

SHAPES AND SIZES

There are so many people these days,
In so many shapes and in so many ways.
They transform themselves to be different
They don't like their shapes or their size
But a fact is like your body
Feet planted firmly on the ground
You can't change what you've already got
Though a fact is a fact and you can't change that.
So why do you need to change your body?

If anybody said, 'What's a shape?'
You would think triangle, square or circle
And if you were asked about size,
You would think triangle, square and circle
But that is not their size
Feet, metres, cm
The point I'm trying to make is that:
Size is size
Shape is shape
Facts are facts
You just can't change the way things are.

Rachael Rowell (12)
Wymondham College

THE RUGBY MATCH

The players all run on the field,
It's England versus Wales,
The captains meet the referee
And toss for heads or tails.

Wales are going to kick off,
It's Humphreys on the ball.
Bayfield's jumped and caught it,
Now they're in a maul.

It is now half time,
England are on twenty.
They have scored four tries,
And Wales haven't scored any!

Then the final whistle sounds.
The score is fifty, twelve.
England have the triple crown.
Another trophy for the shelves.

Charles Pearson (11)
Wymondham College

WILL WE WIN THE FOOTBALL GAME?

We are bottom of the table,
I am watching it on cable.

We are playing the champs,
Who are shining like lamps.

We have not really got a chance,
For them it's just a little dance.

0-7 was the score last season,
I'm sure our team will want to get even.

But after all it's only a game,
Then again, they always put us to shame.

If we were to win,
We would get out the gin.

We would say as we danced through the night,
'We put up a brilliant fright,
to beat the champs who shine like a light.'

Ivan Comer-Moy (12)
Wymondham College

SECRETS OF THE DARK, DARK FOREST

Scary, damp, dark and cold.
are some secrets of the forest that I will tell.

From the second you step in it's cold and damp
and haunted by animals who have died here.
It's dull and quiet, the only thing heard is the crackling
of the leaves while being walked on by small animals and myself.
The evergreen trees seem to tower over me like a skyscraper to an ant.
My only company is myself and small animals who run off into
the haunted, dark shadows when I come near.
The leaves above form a canopy which keeps a lot of the rain out.
My skin tears as I walk past some prickles and catch myself on one.
Animals are running up and down trees collecting food for their winter
hibernation.
Not very often but sometimes I will see a doe run past with her baby.

These are the secrets of the dark, dark forest.

Sarah Jane Cross (12)
Wymondham College

PARANORMAL

Bright lights flashing wildly dancing in the sky,
Try to pretend they're not there just an illusion of the eye,
Green ghostly eyes glittering unnervingly in the night,
Hallowe'en horror and Friday The Thirteenth fright.
Crop circles mysteriously appearing, is it all in your mind?
Moving eyes on paintings and what about slips in time?
Phantom boats with skeleton captain and crew
Ghosts and poltergeists too.
Whispering walls send chills down the spine,
Egyptian scriptures, a long forgotten sign?

Emily Weir (12)
Wymondham College

I DON'T KNOW WHAT TO WRITE

I don't know what to write,
In fact I find it hard
My mum's dusty old birthday cards distract me.

My dad in the lounge watching the boxing,
My mum in the kitchen making us tea.

I've finally got some peace now,
But oh no, my brother has walked in chewing
Skittles as loudly as he can.

I've finally had some ideas which I can jot down,
But my concentration is soon lost because of that
damn clock ticking away nearly bursting my ear.

I'm beginning to get stressed now as I'm ripping apart my paper,
'Right, that's it,' I say and plod up to bed.

Tim Richardson (11)
Wymondham College

WINTER

Winter is a time of year that nobody really likes.
You never see young children riding around on bikes.
The reason for this is of course that it's so cold.
The mystery for this it seems will never, ever unfold.

It always seems to rain or snow
And I don't like it! That's all I know.
I don't think I'll ever understand
That great mystery of this land.

Shaun McKee (12)
Wymondham College

WHY ISN'T THERE PEACE?

In the days of medieval realm,
Where armour was sacred, a sword and helm.
Weapons were crude, made of sticks and stone,
Made for only one purpose, to break people's bones.
Life meant nothing, not even one penny,
The number that were killed was far too many.
First it was the bow and then the gun,
Turning a civilised man into a ravaging one.
It was lambs to the slaughter house, no one cared,
People were intrigued, amazed, scared.
After that the killing machine came,
With six inch armour it was made to kill and maim.
Then the bomb, a murderous thing,
Sorrow to lives they knew it would bring.
Causing carnage to some was like joy to others,
A world peace offering all of which, of course, it smothers.

Adam Oxbury (13)
Wymondham College

A LEAF'S LIFE

As I hang upside down
High up above the ground
I am a lovely colour green
But then I turn to brown
As autumn comes I float down
And now I am on the ground
And if you pick me up and squeeze
I'll make a crunching sound.

Elyse Fitt (11)
Wymondham College

THE PENCIL CASE

In my pencil case it has all the usual things.
A snapped in half 30 cm ruler that can't draw straight lines
and the pencil so blunt it looks as if it was used
to draw the Equator line.
The old tatty rubber that makes a mess when
you scrub out the scrawl in the centre of your page.
The set square which is no longer the right shape,
with the measurements rubbed away and the corner broken off.
The fountain pen that leaks absolutely everywhere
but then it's run out and nobody in the class has a cartridge that fits.
The scissors that are no longer sharp and have chips in
and are so loose that they can't even cut plain paper.
The broken up biro that doesn't fit together,
and is used for other reasons such as firing with.
The compass which is perfect for pricking people,
and it is also good for making marvellously round circles.
Finally the pencil case your pride and joy.
The old tin box which is dented and bashed and has everything written
on it and can stand things from being kicked to being stamped upon.

Robert Watts (12)
Wymondham College

THE SCARECROW

I stand upon a hill
the wind whipping around me.
My clothes are torn and tattered
I've only two bones a stick and a stave
and my one foot is in the grave.
I stand still and lonely on that hill
till I die.

Clare Streel (11)
Wymondham College

THE WAR IS IN MY DREAMS

I had a dream that night
I dreamt I had wings
To fly away from the chaos
The war
The world.
I flew up high
Up to the golden sun
I was with my family again
We played and talked for hours
Till the dark came
I said, 'Goodbye, I will see you again.'
And was pulled
Back down to earth.

I had a nightmare that night
I was in the war of suffering.
Fighting to save our lives.
The bullets
The bombs
Like a lion
Trying to kill its prey
Going off like fireworks -
Lighting the blackest night.
Then it happened
I said, 'Goodbye, I will see you again.'
Then blackness and stars
To my death.

Emily Chalmers (11)
Wymondham College

MY DOG MAX

My dog Max
A fluffy black and white collie
A dog that's loveable
And likes cuddles at the same time.
Hears a crinkle of a crisp packet, *whoosh* and he's there.
Takes food gently, a real gentleman at that.
Also loves chasing pheasants in the fields.
When I'm asleep he's like a soldier on guard at the bottom of the stairs.
Mum says okay you can go and wake him, so he dashes upstairs,
jumping on my bed tickling my ear with his tongue.
Waiting head on side for a bit of bacon sandwich. 'He's not going to
budge Mum!'
My best pal Max even when I'm naughty.

Michael Kerridge (11)
Wymondham College

RACING CARS

Watch all the racing cars,
All ready and lined up.

Red, then green and they're off,
A few don't make it past the line.

In comes a car to the pit,
Everybody rushes to change the tyres.

The first car passes the line,
And the man waves his black and white flag.

All the cars are parked,
And the first three lucky men get their prizes.

Thomas Dring (11)
Wymondham College

THE POPLAR TREES

Oh I do love the poplar trees whispering in the wind.
The tall trees seem to stand guard over Blackthorn throughout the year.
Tall sentries who patter gently when rain is coming.
As the wind howls wildly in the black of midnight you hear them *creak,
creak, creaking,* waving quickly in the gale.

Oh I do love the poplar trees whispering in the wind.
In springtime they put on new green leaves, almost as though they're
celebrating.
Their small rustling leaves can hardly keep quiet.
'Yippee! No more cold winter,' they seem to say.
Little green leaves waving in the breeze, like spinnaker flags at the tops
of tall masts.

Oh I do love the poplar trees whispering in the wind.
In summertime they make small snowstorms of sticky white stuff.
The chickens gobble up the cotton wool fluff.
It covers everything like a veil of poplar wool.
As the trees murmur gently in the breeze the sticky cotton wool seeds
come floating slowly down.

Oh I do love the poplar trees whispering in the wind.
In autumn time the leaves fall gently to the ground, the horses scurry to
hoover them up as they fall to carpet the grass.
The leaves dance, swirling on the wind, leaping and pirouetting like any
wild dancer, finally settling reluctantly to the ground after one last twirl,
flying on the wind.

Oh I do love the poplar trees whispering in the wind.
In wintertime they stand tall and bare, lean gaunt skeletons, whipped by
the gale.
Long bony branches twisted by the wind, then as the wind dies down,
they stand, alone and quiet, still against the fading light, splendid old
sentries in the dying sun.

Oh I do love the poplar trees whispering in the wind.
They're always there, part of my life.
Those trees stand there, spring, summer, autumn and winter.
The wind blows by, the sun rises and sinks, the poplar trees stand sentry
over Blackthorn Farm, they've been there all my life.

Jamie Walker (11)
Wymondham College

THE FIRE

I was sitting in my armchair sipping a can of coke, whilst watching
telly, I heard a roaring sound and then a ripping sound and then my
Aunt Ellie got up to see what these noises were.
She opened the door, and flames burst out and Aunt fell to the floor at
the disastrous roar.
She got up and screamed then ran out of the house.
I reached for the phone in a panic, I punched in as quickly as possible
the numbers 999 then asked for the Fire Service.
I got up, snatched the cat from the rug, made for the front door and
burst out into the crowd watching the smoke bellowing from our
windows.
The fire was flickering its deadly flames around the house.
I then heard a deafening siren and saw the huge, red truck fly around the
corner and halt at the sight of the flames.
Four men jumped out in smart uniform and bright yellow helmets and
grabbed the hose and dragged it along the ground.
Not before long, the fire was put out and there were just puffs of
lingering smoke.
Most of our belongings were wrecked and so was our house. The fire
was now dead.

Morgan Stiefel (14)
Wymondham College

SQUIRTING RAINBOWS

Bare legs.
Bare toes.
Paddling pool.
Garden hose.
Daisies sprinkled
In the grass.
Dandelions
Bold as brass.
Squirting rainbows,
Sunbeam flashes
Backyard's full
Of shrieks and splashes.

Christian Rayner (12)
Wymondham College

FOOTBALL

Football is a sportsman's game
Even if you cry on the floor
When you get a bit injured
You make it look much more

It's always great to score a goal
Even better if you win
But if you hack and get sent off
You'll be sent in the sin bin

When the referee shouts foul
You pretend that you don't hear
As that red card in his pocket
Is your deepest fear.

Daniel Woodrow (12)
Wymondham College

TREE LIFE

Over there stands the old, grand tree,
Standing straight and tall
The ivy coils around the trunk,
And creepy creatures crawl.
Ladybirds with spotted satchels
Resting on their backs.
Earwigs with their sharp-like pincers
Threatening like that.
In winter,
Freezing cold,
Snow rests gently on the branches,
Melting.
Afternoon sunbeams slowly enhancing the tree.
Grey and red creatures,
Come out to play.
In the intense summer light.
Looking for their nutty cuisine.
Bolting away
Predators come
Birds big and small
Proudly perch on the arm of the evergreen
Sheltered from the storm
Next . . .
When you look at that old grand tree
Just imagine how many creatures there could be.

Amy Hodson (11)
Wymondham College

THE STALLION

As if from nowhere he appeared,
Galloping down the rocky hillside,
Ready to face his challenge,
Over the moor and onwards he galloped,
To where a fellow stallion waited,
He pawed the ground angrily
Impatient for the fight to start,
Together they reared,
And thrashed out wildly,
There was a muffled thud,
As the stallion's body hit the floor,
He groaned and took one last breath,
Before lying still,
But every night
There is a sound of hoof beats,
For the stallion still gallops on,
And forever will.

Fiona McDonell (13)
Wymondham College

NIGHT-TIME

Silently so no one can hear,
Footsteps getting louder and louder,
I'm so scared I could freeze with fear.
I'm still asleep and the doorknob turns.
The church bell sounds loud and clear.
I see a white figure entering my room,
And hear footsteps very near.
I see a white face in front of me
And . . . *Boo!* It's all a dream.

Mary van Beuningen (11)
Wymondham College

DUSK

Dusk is like an autumn leaf,
A golden sun orange with tints of yellow,
It hovers above the green meadows,
The sky darkens to a musty grey.

Tree trunks turn into ghostly figures,
As the ground sucks in the red sun,
A glowing sky remains that slowly fades away,
A dark moonlit sky with twinkling stars above,
Not a cloud in sight,
The now replaced ball glowing a solemn white,
Which was once a golden orange ball.

Both like ping-pong balls,
Stuck in the sky,
What would happen if they fell?
Day would be night,
But night would have no moon,
Darkness forever,
The black never dies out.

Laura Sidwell (14)
Wymondham College

THE GARDEN

The grass as fresh as a ripened lemon sways beneath my feet
It looks so sharp, but if you feel, it's soft, gentle and sweet.
Pretty little daisies blowing in the zephyr
Each and every petal as light as a smooth, white feather
I lower myself into the grass, looking at the sky
Thinking, wondering, How? When? Why?

Tara Kane (13)
Wymondham College

OUR HARRY

Under the dappled blue sky, in the light breeze it stood,
people stare and scream but I don't see why they should.
Why should they? He's only a Bigfoot all scared and alone,
it's not as if they'll use him for a big scary clone.
He's so friendly, cute, sweet, and funny,
if a bee stings him, his eyes will go runny.
I feel sorry for him I really do,
yet I don't know what to do.
He'll make a great husband to the right girl,
she'll wear a green dress with a blue dapple swirl.
We love him and we always will, just like a brother,
the first time she saw him, he frightened my mother.
We know our Harry is a bit mad,
we couldn't live without him that would be really bad.

Daniela Waters (14)
Wymondham College

THE BOMB SHELTER

As I ran through the sea of glass
And people losing blood as I pass
The siren which is weakening as bombs come down.
As I pass there is the shelter not far off.
Nearly there now there is a bogeyman!
Quick hide!
It's too late they see me!
Bang! Bang!
Small silver pellets come whistling through the air
The pain, *ow!* The pain is really bad
And then fell to the ground it was so near but so far away.

Edward Olding (11)
Wymondham College

SCHOOLDAY

Walk in quietly they shout,
And tuck your shirt in Mr Brown,
Right, today class,
'Come on Miss hurry up
Right detention after school and don't be late.'
As the bell goes, she collects in our homework.
'Come back Colin Crew, where's your homework?'
'I'm sorry Miss, but, but my dog ate it Miss.'
'That's no excuse Colin Crew,
First thing tomorrow morning otherwise it's
A red card for you.'
'OK Miss. I'm very sorry Miss.'
As I walk to my next lesson I'm as
nervous as a wreck.
But now it's lunchtime, I've got PE next
I've got a bleep test next!

I'm at PE, I've forgotten my trainers.
'Excuse me Sir, I'm very sorry, but I haven't
got my trainers Sir.'
'And why not?'
'Well my dog ate them sir!'
'Well you will have to run in bare feet
then, won't you young man!'
'Yes Sir!'

PE's over now, and so is school, my feet are sore
So off I go home after another day.
Goodbye school, see you another day!'

Zoë Norman (13)
Wymondham College

SEASONS

Like a burst of colour flowing on to the empty canvas,
Like a comet ablaze appearing through the open sky,
Like a light flooding into the black atmosphere;

Spring

Like a fire flaming bright, burning thoughts out, away,
Like the stars, shining aglow, a picture of joy on their faces,
Like a chemical reaction, fizzing and bursting with ecstatic life;

Summer

Like a washed away castle built upon the sandy beach,
Like glowing embers, lost from the blazing fire,
Like a washed out cloth, drained of all its colour;

Autumn

Like the dying beast, withering its last breath away,
Like the hand of death, grasping a withered limb in its paralysing claw,
Like the frozen fate that seeks to seal the tomb;

Winter

Tom Hilton (14)
Wymondham College

IN THE DEAD OF WINTER

In the dead of Winter
A cruel wind swept the forest
Like a thousand spirits seeking revenge
It squealed through the trees trying to avenge.

A small mound had risen covered by silky leaves.
As the leaves blew away a corpse lay there
But with no hands in the sleeves.
The sickening image vanished and turned in my head
Then everything went dead.

Austen Williams (13)
Wymondham College

BUTTERCUP LANE

Down Buttercup Lane the air is fresh and sweet smelling,
It is a story book blooming with life.
Hundreds of golden buttercups line the cobble-stoned lane
And drift far off into the fields.
Bees buzz around and lazily fly to and from their hives.

The cobble-stoned lane shines
And it feel like a fairy tale.
The dew rests on the long blades of grass,
Glistens on the soft sunlight
And looks like pearls scattered around the fields.

The trees in Buttercup Lane are alive.
They dance in the wind
And hum a soft tune
While the bees buzz in harmony
And the birds sing a sweet melody
There is music down Buttercup Lane.

Buttercup Lane is perfect
Nothing seems out of place
Everything fits together
To form Buttercup Lane . . .

Gemma E McKay
Wymondham College

The Lonely Child

The
lonely
child
sat sitting
lost and
lonely
in a darkened
room.

The moonlight
shined in
highlighting her massive,
blue staring
eyes.
The Only
Sound
was of
her parents
fighting
in the next room
She sat on
her bed
hoping,
waiting for
the shouting
to stop.
She heard a banging of a door.
Her
eyes widened
in terror
as her father
stepped towards her

With an
evil
glint
in
his
eyes!

Emily Humphrey (13)
Wymondham College

SPRING

The sun arises
a pale misty sky awakes
as it turns into another spring day,
rabbits are jumping
birds are singing
on a misty spring day.

Doors are opening now
people are out and about
children are playing
in the damp soft fields
on a misty spring day.

It's getting dark
and the animals close their eyes,
everything silent
at the end of the day
waiting for another
spring day to begin.

Ella Howell (11)
Wymondham College

THE SOUNDS OF WAR

The sounds of war are the most mentally disturbing sounds I have ever
heard.
They haunt you forever.
Constantly ringing through you mind over and over again.
You're reminded of the sound of your best friend,
dying in your arms right before your eyes.
You're reminded of the Spitfires whistling as they nosedive out of the
sky,
You're reminded of the blast of the bomb when nearly all your team got
blown into pieces.
Pieces that my eyes could not bear to look at.
With these pictures in my mind which are slowly falling to pieces in my
mind,
I will bring myself closer to the conclusion of suicide,
And going to heaven or hell to join my well-missed war friends.
But every time I go to do it I think how lucky I am to still be alive.

Richard Dunsire (13)
Wymondham College

A POEM ABOUT NOTHING

Tears had filled my broken eyes
My mind had screamed my voice had died.
My body numb my teeth like spears,
Black and blue were all my fears.

This living hell no place for me,
Each day would take a century
There was no way out all doors were locked,
All signs of love and care were blocked.

I thought of golden magic days,
Those thoughts were cleared and others stayed
I look for dreams to make me smile
To find those dreams I looked for miles.

These mumbled words don't have a meaning,
But every line, describes my feelings.

Kirsty Alston (13)
Wymondham College

STRANGE

The moonlight glistening on the surface of the water,
The trees swaying in the wind,
The mysterious air clinging round me,
The smoke from a far away bonfire,
All seem strange to me.

The silvery stars twinkling in the dark sky,
The squawk of birds as they settle down for the night,
The curiosity I have to explore this wonderful land,
The dew on the grass,
All seem strange to me.

In the silence,
A crack, pop and a scuttle,
It startles me,
My heart is nearly coming out of my mouth,
The chills of fear running down my spine,
I see a black cat run in front of me,
My nerves calm,
I am relaxed,
But they still all seem strange to me.

Beth Riley (12)
Wymondham College

HALLOWE'EN

It's Hallowe'en!
Children come running out from
their houses.
Dressed up as witches and ghouls,
With pumpkins that glow in the
October night.

Knock. knock!
As they bang on the door of an old
woman's house,
Saying trick or treat,
The old woman gave the children
some sweets,
Then they all ran off with a smile.

Melissa Gamble (13)
Wymondham College

EVIL!

It came alive with eyes of *fire*,
It stared at me burning me with its gaze,
I tried to run but I could not move,
It was descending on me like an eagle catching prey.
I was scared, I was freaked,
There was no word to describe the fear,
Suddenly I could move.
I ran, ran like an arrow piercing the air.
I looked round, it was gone,
I started to run again,
But I fell, fell into its realm,
I tried to escape, but I was trapped,
Trapped for life.

Benedict McLernan (12)
Wymondham College

190

SCHOOL DINNERS

Trays cluttering, people shouting ready to eat the *horrid* school
dinners,
They chuck the mouldy, blue eggs in the corroding bowl,
With the hairy smelly earwigs in the apple ready to attack,
School dinners I *hate* them!

If you ask for more they will tell you to sweep the floor and never ask
again,
But remember if you eat the uncooked chips you will most probably die
of school poison,
Or the pink, bony chicken will most probably make you hair fall out,
School dinners I *hate* them!

So I will only tell you once *never eat school dinners!* (If you
can help it)

Alice Rogers (13)
Wymondham College

VIEW ACROSS MY MOUNTAIN

I trek up to my mountain top every night to relax
and take my worries away. My mountain over
looks a lake, my mountain overlooks my house.
Where I lay every night I leave an engraving of
my shape, as I lie on my back facing the darkening
light, dreaming of what the next day will bring. As
it gets dark and the stars brighten and the moon
appears I wait for a shooting star to wish upon.
I leave at nine sharp and brush my hair with a piece
of bark because I made a date with a mate.

Robert Smithers (13)
Wymondham College

HOPE

Loneliness is fear
Fear is unhappiness
Unhappiness is crying
Crying is sadness
Sadness is all around us
All around us is mankind

Friends with us is joyfulness
Joyfulness is happiness
Happiness is laughing
Laughing is hope
Hope is all around us
All around us is mankind

Alanna Stibbons (13)
Wymondham College

THE FOUR SEASONS

The beautiful colours of spring fill me full of joy,
The fabulous scent of flowers makes the world go by.

The warm air of summer makes everyone seem so happy,
The heat of the sun makes everyone a fiery red or a golden brown.

The golden leaves of autumn crunch beneath my feet,
The chill wind of autumn rustles up my hair.

The crystal snow of winter melts beneath my feet,
Which lets me know that Christmas is near,
With lots of special treats.

Bryony Jaques (13)
Wymondham College

THE VICTIM

Wild fierce howling winds blew the hunted trees
Grow in darkness poisonous plant breed
Rain plumage's heavy sounds
Wet and damp mud tracks collide the ground

Slowly and nervously on the alert
The young and newly born investigates the space
Step by step the twigs snapped like bangers
Stopping to peer at every little sound

Slowly it crept along the broken path
Eyes fixed on every position happening around
Searching its empty mind for when to approach
Sudden and swift the action
Red blood around its mouth.

Matthew Eckles (14)
Wymondham College

THE MOONLIGHT

The shiny, glittering stream which sits all alone,
Twinkles in the moonlight with nowhere to go.
She sits and stares at the stars as if they were her night light,
Whilst the moon glares and shivers with fright.

As down from the sky comes massive illuminated flashes,
The stream tries to hide in the moons shallow light.
With no success she travels down stream,
To find peace and silence that she always needs.

Kelly Foyster (13)
Wymondham College

MY FAVOURITE PLACE

The soft sound of the little humming
bird was a lovely wake up call to start
the day.
The unbelievable view from the
mountain tops took me by surprise.
I never thought it would look this
beautiful.
I went near the edge but I couldn't fall
because there were tall black barriers
guarding it,
The drop was an intensely far way
down.
I couldn't look for long.

Claire Roberts (13)
Wymondham College

A HOUSE

A house stood a couple of yards away from the road,
The gate shattering throughout the years,
The rough flint walls stood tough and clear,
And the lower part of the house was not to be seen.
For the grass was as long as it could be,
Had never been cut at any degree.

The home belonged to an old couple,
Sweet but quiet throughout their wisest years,
For one bright day the time will come
The old shattered house will be gone,
And a new life will be built.

Louise Wain (11)
Wymondham College

THE BEACH

The soft sand ran gently through my toes like
the trickle of a brook running steadily through
the mountains.
The warm summer's sun beamed down on my
Freckled skin, making me feel cosy and warm
Inside.
The gentle pounding of the ocean smacking
against some sharp rocks echoed in the distance.

I could smell the strong aroma of salt, I could
even taste it.
Seagulls swarmed around me, swooping for my
fresh sandwiches and screeching like 100 life-
guards whistles sounding for attention.
People were splashing about in the warm sea.
Some were just lazily sunbathing, lapping up the
gorgeous sun.

Others were crabbing off the brutal rocks, close
to the fun-filled pier, which was producing a
sweet, sickening smell from the candy-floss shop.
All was calm and peaceful on that beach.
'Child drowning! Quick! Help!'
I heard someone scream as they came desperately
running up the beach.

Marina Thomas (13)
Wymondham College

LIFE

I have a dog, she was white, fluffy and full of life, but
now she's old and tired, she sleeps
All
Day.

Sometimes
I walk in and
Stare
At her
For a moment to see if she's
Breathing . . . she is
But only just.

She hobbles along
Like a penguin on ice.
She only does this
When she has her tea
Or
Goes to the toilet.

She's 15 now
And about to go to doggy heaven
Just two more days says the vet,
Only two more days . . .

In a way it's the best thing to do,
But I'm gonna miss her.
She's older than I am and that's old,
But everything has to go eventually,
It's natural, even you will have to go some time!

And that's life!

Edward Rout (14)
Wymondham College

THE SEA

Crash! The first wave hits the rocks,
Clouds like monsters, mysterious and dark.
The sea darts in and out of the caves
Then the rain starts to fall . . .

Trees shake and swirl in the wind
Trying to get free, away from the storm.
Their movements complicated and full of rhythm
Then the rain starts to fall.

Birds swooping, sweeping in the sky
Singing songs of uppermost joy.
Nose-diving to catch their prey
Then the rain starts to fall.

Calling upon the emptiness of the forgotten storm
Rain falling, like the tears of an unhappy child.
Morbid feelings all around
Then the sun starts to shine . . .

Kathryn Bloom (13)
Wymondham College

THE CREEPY LIGHT OF MYSTERY

I was walking through the dark, creepy forest suddenly I glimpsed a
light which was getting clearer to my eye, it made me shudder.
I wasn't moving my body and my eyes were fixed on the light.
It got bigger and bigger until I could nearly touch it.
I didn't see it because it died down gradually like it suddenly had
no strength in it then it went like a big mystery.

Luke Plumridge (11)
Wymondham College

FIREWORKS

They rise like sudden fiery flowers
That burst upon the night.
Then fall to earth in burning showers
Of crimson, blue and white.

Like buds too wonderful to name.
Each miracle unfolds.
And Catherine Wheels begin to flame
Like whirling marigolds.

Rockets and Roman candles make
an orchard of the sky.
Whence magic trees their petals shake
Upon each gazing eye.

Rachel Stroud (13)
Wymondham College

THE SIREN

The siren wails at half-past eight
I stoop out of bed half awake
I clamber down
stairs in an awful
state
Then hurtle across the dark green grass
I trip and hit some blood thirsty glass
Lying there as stiff as a rock
Never to see light
only dark

Elisabeth Godsill (11)
Wymondham College

THE HORSE

At the hour of midnight
I hoped that I would see it
Its golden mane
Shines and gleams
And its smooth body
Soft to the touch
Who owns it
Nobody knows
Suddenly I see a glimpse of gold
There it goes
Then when I look up it's gone
So quickly
So fast
I won't see it again tonight.

Charlotte Beaumont (11)
Wymondham College

WINTER CHANGES TO SPRING

Spring is here,
Winter has gone,
No more ice on the ground,
Daffodils dancing in the breeze,
The bulbs come up,
The snow goes down,
Children playing in the street,
Laughter and happiness,
Everywhere,
The coldness has gone,
The warmth is here,
No more hats, scarves or coats.

Felicity Hesse (11)
Wymondham College

FROSTY NIGHT

The crisp moonlight beams
along the grasses frosty seams.
The air is strangely cool
and the wind tangles like wool.
A mystery howl is heard
it does not disturb the bird.
The stars sparkle brightly
and ice warriors march mightily.
A candle light glimmers softly
near a shadow very ghostly.
Underneath the ground
there is not a little sound.
The stars sparkle
the moon is bright,
The air is cool
it's a frosty night.

Sarah O'Donnell (12)
Wymondham College

SHIPWRECK

Deep at the bottom of the seabed
An ancient, rotting shipwreck lies
It's been there for one hundred years
All around the turquoise sea sighs.

Nobody has ever been there
Right down there at the bed
Smelly, rotting, ancient
Like the brain in a dead man's head.

A discovery has been made
An amber chest covered in brown, wet and mould
Everyone is excited
Treasure is found, silver and gold!

Deep at the bottom of the seabed
An ancient, rotting shipwreck lies
Been there for one hundred years
All around the sea sighs.

Alice Crosby (12)
Wymondham College

MYSTERY

As I come outside from my warm house,
I see the moon wink at me
I look around and I see through
the fog and it is
a mouse squealing at me.
I hear a laugh and look up
And there it is, it flies across
the moon.
A witch on a broomstick holding
a spoon.
Smoke running after it,
With moonlight on its tail.
Miracles, enchantment has happened in one night
So why don't you go to bed
And snuggle down tight
So the next morning you hopefully
will be all right.

Kym Haverson (13)
Wymondham College

LOST IN SPACE

Stars, Planets, the Sun,
All magnificently bright,
Saturn with its beautiful painted rings,
The Moon grey and white with craters like cups.

Stars as bright as day
The Sun with hot, dancing flames licking at you
like a fire.

Pluto like an Antarctic out in space, a frozen
desert of ice and rock, a planet miles away.

Mars as red as wine with exploding volcanoes
like cannonballs coming at you.

The Milky Way as white as ivory,
And the black hole as black as midnight.

Back to earth at night, where the moon is
shining bright.

Louisa Butcher (11)
Wymondham College

VOICE OF THE DAY

The day starts the world is silent
At 7 o'clock the day draws on,
At 8 o'clock the dreaming stops
At 9 o'clock no one wakes up!
Little Tom starts to rise not a sound for he never cries
He quietly steps out of his cot and looks out of the window
He sees the street below, quiet, silent nothing moves.

Martyn Cook (11)
Wymondham College

THAT NIGHT

That night,
the stars shone like a million catseyes,
embedded in the sky,
shining gold
a beauty there for all to behold.

That night,
the wispy smoke curled and danced,
around the bonfire,
shining gold,
enticing to all who saw it, young and old.

That night,
the evil souls shrieked and darted
underneath the moon
glistening bold
death to all, who dare behold.

Alice McConnell (13)
Wymondham College

THE BUTTERFLY

The butterfly, the flutterby,
So delicate and fine.
Symmetrical in every way,
Each pattern and each line.

The flutterby, the butterfly,
Her tiny feet that tickle.
Butterfly knows what she likes,
She isn't fickle.

Elizabeth Bayliss (12)
Wymondham College

OUR HOLIDAY

The family needed a holiday,
Where we should go that's the thing,
We all had lots of ideas but,
Where to go,
What to buy
What to bring.

Victoria and George said the seaside,
Dad said he needed the sun and to lie,
Mum said how about America again?
Grandad said must I fly?

Nanny said she would just love it,
In a house with a lovely big pool,
Dad said he wanted a nice car to drive,
Grandad was left out on a stool.

We all enjoyed the journey,
Because it was fun but far too long,
It's really great when you get there,
We were happy and all sang a song.

When we arrived at a villa,
I went to look at my bed,
Dad went to check the TV set
Grandad still wants to be fed.

Victoria Coe (11)
Wymondham College

THE DEADLY LAKE

The frost was dripping from the trees
And the wind was whipping my legs
Swirling like a swarm of bees
Stinging and scratching my bare face

I strode forward into the storm
The rain planting daggers in my eyes
I knew I had to reach the girl
Before it was too late.

I stumbled over a log
Reaching out desperately with my hands
I was falling, falling down
Into space beyond

The hollow space was filled with mist
It swallowed me up and choked me
I was bitten with a frigid feeling
As I hit the water

The force of the fall stung my cheeks
And I struggled to stay afloat
But the water dragged me down
And the weeds entwined themselves around my arms and legs.

And there I shall stay
Until time has been forgotten
Frozen into place
On the lake's bed.

Sarah Kate Jones (12)
Wymondham College

THE TOOTH FAIRY

Little girl with curly hair,
Flying in the night
Pearly teeth and blue eyes,
With a perfect bite.

Underneath your pillow lies,
A tiny little tooth
In it weeks of wiggling
Until the tooth came loose.

Where does that tiny tooth go?
Maybe underground
Are there hills of shining munchers?
Are there piles of pounds?

Is there a castle built of teeth?
Are there dragons' lairs?
If a dragon chips a tooth
Does he use the spares?

Does the tooth-queen wear a crown
Made of teeth and gold?
Do the fairies sleep by day?
Do *they* do as they're told?

All this I used to think about
While lying in my bed,
Until my older sister said
It was my mum instead.

Laura Seymour (13)
Wymondham College

I Treasure True Love

He stood there alone when I first saw him.
I watched and stared I thought about him all day and all night.
He wasn't cute or even very nice . . .
But there was that *thing*.
I wrote him a letter and his reply was so stimulating,
It proved how intellectual he was
I kept asking myself , am I in love?

The gleam in his eye was heart-pounding,
But why did I like him!
Was it his charm? Or his personality!
Or just his pure intelligence that flowed like a waterfall
each time the conversation broke out?
When we are together we are inseparable - but why?
How long will this last?
Who knows! But while we are like this
Let us enjoy it . . .
I treasure true love!

Michelle Kimber (13)
Wymondham College

Hedgehogs

Small, spiky and round
They move slowly and quietly across the ground
Moving through the crispy leaves
Underneath the swaying trees
Crawling through the darkness on their tiny feet
Never knowing exactly what they will meet
As morning comes they crawl away
Then they sleep again through another day.

Laura Betts (12)
Wymondham College

DAD

Bump into my Dad and you will see
A man of lots of love and caring,
Who spends his whole life sharing.
He may have small light-blue eyes, bad dress sense and be fat.
But is there anything wrong with that?
He is a policeman at Wymondham
He keeps the streets safe at night
Then he goes to bed and sleeps tight
He has very short brown hair.
I hope it grows back but he doesn't care,
His hobbies are fishing, trains and tele
That's why he has such a big belly,
So to sum up my Dad
I hope you all agree
He ain't half bad . . . !

Scott Taylor (13)
Wymondham College

KEY

A key is an answer to never be told,
Think of the peace that it would unfold
The war, the crime, the killing in cities
Wouldn't it be nice if someone took pity.
The key to freedom we all know is there
What about us, you and me, nobody cares.

Philippa Ball (12)
Wymondham College

ARGUMENTS

When I look into those mysterious beady eyes,
I can tell there's something terribly wrong.
What have I done now? I ask suspiciously,
Was it this, was it that? No, nothing!
Then she widens her dangerously loaded mouth ,
And blasts out colonies of nonsense.
It wasn't me, it was someone else, I beg.
But still it comes, firing down at me,
And only me alone, nobody else there to help.
Now I see, a mist of overcoming magic,
Wonderfully falling on to my puzzled head.
Total forgiveness for all that I *haven't* done.
But still, I repeat, it wasn't me - honestly,
Oh well! Mistakes will always be made.

Hannah Blagnys (13)
Wymondham College

THE SEASIDE SHARK

I watch the fat man floating out to sea
The shark looking for its tea.
Slipping under him silently
The man now starting to swim violently.
The shark now swimming in on its prey.
The man is having his last day.
He panics and starts to kick
But still goes down like a tonne of bricks.
His blood and water start to merge
The man will never again be seen or heard.

James Leech
Wymondham College

THE LATEST CRAZE

Up, down, circles around, swings and loops the loop
The yo-yo coils up like a hedgehog rolls up in a ball
The brave bungee-jumper sails down through the air
Many tricks to learn, *walking the dog, rocking the baby*
What can you do with yours?
There are wooden ones, plastic, even mechanised with flashing lights
Pogs, sticker books and virtual pets, but this craze just has to be the best
When this one dies down there'll be a new craze next term
Then we'll have it all again.
I wonder what it will be next time, juggling balls perhaps.

Laura Beth Mitchell-Hynd (13)
Wymondham College

THE WOMAN IN THE STREET

I was walking down the street and there she was,
Spread out across the pavement - all shrivelled up.
I concentrated on the situation ahead of me and it was a problem,
Not only did I have to help her but I had fallen in love with her.

Her eyes were sea-blue and her hair brown, like silk,
I stared into her deep blue eyes and it was like a whirlpool.
I was attracted to her and I couldn't get away because of the power
It was like a force that pushed me towards her
My conscience said 'No! don't get sucked in.'

I picked her up and carried her over to shelter.
A few sprinkles of water landed on her head.
It woke her up within an instance
She looked at me and smiled and said 'Thank you.'

Mark Hollis (13)
Wymondham College

MUM

As the knife slips
From the grasp of the red
Tired, wrinkled hands
The sound of the stainless steel knife
Clashing with the ceramic plate
Fills my ears.

I can see the sigh in
Her eyes
And the exhausted look on her face
Shows through her tinted
Mask of skin
Then her smooth radiant nose emerges into a tissue.

I can see the pain inside
Maybe the recent death in the family
Has made an affect on her
Slim but tired body.
It's her birthday tomorrow
Maybe that has added more concern to the dispute.

As another year passes by
I ask myself
Why the depressed, lonely
Stressful face!
Is it guilt or fate?
That, I'll never know . . .

Scott Taplin (13)
Wymondham College

MY GRAN

We walked into the room
and there she lay - fast asleep.
You could see she was in pain.
Leslie her friend tried to smile
but his pain and worry stopped him.
The drip bag by her bed was getting
fuller and fuller.
It wasn't very nice.
Her pale face hanging off her bones.
I had to look away when I saw the tubes
in her elbow and nose.
When she awoke she did nothing but complain
She said that none of this will help her.
We decided to leave as my Dad was getting upset.
He couldn't cope with Mother's disease . . .

Dobyn Lowe (13)
Wymondham College

HOMELESS

Homeless children everywhere
On the streets of London
Where they come from no-one cares.
On the streets of London
Dark and dismal faces stare
On the streets of London
They sit and wait in despair
On the streets of London . . .

James Dicks (13)
Wymondham College

THE MISSING SUMMER

This year, summer stayed well hidden all year long.
The flowers failed to blossom and the birds refused to sing their song.
The months passed by and winter proudly stepped in.
It took the non-existent summers place as if it were extinct.
Now Christmas is coming and the sun has still not shone.
As the special place reserved for summer has quickly been and gone.
So summer's missed its chance to brighten up our days.
The days are short and the nights are long - much to our dismay.
As soon as school is over, dark starts to descend.
The cold weather, the wind and the rain
it's enough to drive you round the bend.
So all I'm asking is 'Please make us happy,
we simply want to have some sun.'
For all we need to make us smile
is to have a little fun . . .

Sarah Kitchen (13)
Wymondham College

AUTUMN

The leaves go a crusty mustard brown
And they eventually start to fall down.
Trees still sway in the autumn breeze
People get colds and start to sneeze.
The trees look dark and shaded in front of the beautiful sunset red.
People snuggle up under their winter duvets in their warm soft beds.

Katie van Beuningen (13)
Wymondham College

UNTITLED

Mother Earth cries, she is bleeding all over with cuts and grazes
and has been beaten and pricked - which has resulted in bruises.

She tells us and shouts, but we never seem to listen, we ignore her
pleads and hurt her some more.

We cut down her rainforests, to make her go bald. We build heavy
dense buildings, which cut into her skin like a sharpened dough-
cutter embedded, which leaves an imprint when gone. We inject
her veins and arteries with pollution and junk with plastic *cola*
bottles and packets of crisps. We have taken off her hat, her sunscreen,
her ozone protection, we have let the suns rays come in and burn her.

We dig up her tissue, for stuff to eat. We pluck out her hair when we're
bored on the pitch. We have done everything possible to torture her
so much.

But she still lets us live with her water and animals.

So why are we trying to kill her off?

Without her we'd die, without us - we would live . . .
So why are we trying to kill her off?
Let's try and pay her back - let's give her a hug.
So let's start with putting bandages on her, and giving her stitches,
let's give her, her sunscreen, her hat, and her big white smile back . . .

Sara Helmi (13)
Wymondham College

FOUR SEASONS

First of all comes spring.
A time for new life and new things.
Yellow daffodils blowing in the breeze
New-born lambs, jumping about in fresh pastures
And a chick, just hatching from an egg.

Then it's time for summer.
Clear blue skies and a blazing sun.
The excitement of going on holiday
The sea and sand at the beach,
And ice-cream melting, all too quick.

Autumn, means back to school.
Golden leaves falling to the ground
Leaving bare trees behind.
Shiny conkers, their shells containing silk linings,
And now it's showing signs of winter.

Winter is the last season.
With snowflakes falling to the ground.
And an icy cold frost.
Then Christmas with decorations and presents
And finally spring comes again . . .

Hannah Martin (13)
Wymondham College

THE ACTOR

The rumbling of drums
Signals their entrance.
Music begins from a shrouded place
Everybody is washed with wonder
Awaiting an unknown face.

The pinnacle of the orchestra's performance.
Is drawing near - you can feel it!
You're looking left and right
For someone to appear on the stage
Then the band reaches it.

Crash! The cymbals meet!

A figure - lean and tall
From the right, runs onto the stage.
His clothes in character;
Crimson and yellow,
Silver and beige.

Playing the part of someone he knows not
Someone most probably contrary to him.
Someone whose manner is vaguely suited to his own
For he must obey their every whim.

The portrayal he is obeying
Has control over his every move.
He is a puppet on a string
And I wish someday . . . I could be just like him!

Jade Maddocks (13)
Wymondham College

WINTER

Wind blowing in my face
Ice and frost on the ground
Nights get cold each day
Thousands of people in hats and scarves
Every night the sky gets darker and darker
Rolling up balls ready for a fright
See the frost countryside
Now every fire is burning in the street
Icy-cold mornings
Ground covered in frost and ice
How many people wrap up warm
The hillsides covered in snow
See the frosty streets that children play in
Winter is the coldest season ever.

Kirsty Collins (11)
Wymondham College

THE CAVERN

Here in the cavern all damp and cold,
I walk alone in dim candlelight,
The ghosts and spirits of people long ago,
Haunt and possess this deep chamber,
I can hear the voices of Romans,
Whispering and planning their next attack.
Trickling water leaves crystals in its wake
And water from a stalactite drips
Monotonously
As I leave the cavern,
I say goodbye to a strange, mystical world.

Laura Howes (13)
Wymondham College